Magic and Loss

Magic and Loss

In letters to his young daughter, a father,
suddenly facing death, rediscovers life.

Greg Raver Lampman

HAMPTONROADS
PUBLISHING COMPANY, INC.

For information write:

Hampton Roads Publishing Company, Inc.
891 Norfolk Square
Norfolk, VA 23502

Or call: (804) 459-2453
FAX: (804) 455-8907

If you are unable to order this book from your local
bookseller, you may order directly from the publisher.
Quantity discounts for organizations are available.
Call 1-800-766-8009, toll-free.

ISBN 1-57174-015-5 (paper)
ISBN 1-57174-017-1 (cloth)

10 9 8 7 6 5 4 3 2 1

Printed on acid-free paper in the United States of America

Author's Note

In some corner of our psyche, we all believe we are immortal. This belief persists although we *know,* intellectually, that we are all terminal, drawn from the moment of our birth toward extinction.

In American culture, though, we prefer not to ponder tragedy, suffering, and death. We worship *life*—health foods, jogging, youth, vitality, medical miracles. We believe sickness, death—even—age can be thwarted with cryogenics, the right faith, technology, or medical treatment.

We draw comfort from books that suggest that life progresses in an orderly fashion, from birth through childhood, through marriage, through middle age, through our final years where, presumably, death arrives as a relief.

Many people, especially those of my generation, whom some called "baby boomers," work to avoid "premature death," as if death, too, should operate on a timetable, wait in the wings for its cue. Meanwhile, they fight furiously the signs of aging—baldness, wrinkles, fat—as if these reminders of mortality were simply cosmetic changes in an otherwise changeless body.

When forced to face mortality, in friends or loved ones, too many of us distance ourselves from sorrows of the human condition by blaming those who suffer. We feel relief when a person diagnosed with lung cancer had a history of smoking. Many blame AIDS victims for their promiscuity, and heart attack victims for eating fatty foods or living stressful lives. In doing so, we place the sick and the dying in categories to which we don't belong, building walls between ourselves and thoughts of our own mortality.

When asked how we wish to die, most answer the same:

suddenly, with no suffering, preferably during sleep. This is the dream of dying while still avoiding real confrontation with mortality.

My own confrontation stunned me, coming when it seemed I was far too young, 37, with a rewarding career, a loving marriage, and a recently-adopted daughter.

In the spring of 1992, I suffered a seizure. In months that followed, doctors learned that I suffer from an illness that, almost invariably, is terminal.

With the seizures, a trap door flew open. My life went into a free fall. My sense of despair and powerlessness reminded me of myths about protagonists hurled into the netherworld to encounter monsters, blackness, and rivers of death. Sometimes, the hero returns with a sacred object or lesson. Sometimes the hero dies.

As I was thrown into this medical netherworld, friends, relatives, co-workers, medical personal, even relative strangers, showered me with books, anecdotes, magazine articles, medical reports they thought would be helpful. Some stories or articles or books detailed the benefits of herbal treatments, homeopathic medicines, vitamin C, laughter, or the "right" attitude. I stocked my library with books written by survivors of their illnesses: books to help people beat colon cancer, AIDS. In many, authors boasted of finding cures ignored by the medical profession.

These accounts offered me scant comfort. In these books, victors wrote about their victories often years after their diseases were conquered. I wondered: What about that vast majority for whom there are no miracles or secret cures? How can one confront mortality when there are no easy answers?

In emphasizing cures, miracles, and "oursmarting" doctors, these books tended to skirt the toughest issues. They fail to convey the sense of terror and helplessness. At the same time, they fail to capture moments of pure exhilaration and insight that surprisingly emerge.

In my own confrontation with mortality, something inconceivable became conceivable, something intolerable became tolerable, something utterly meaningless showed the way to deeper meaning.

Few around me seemed to appreciate that life's final passage—a journey beginning after a pronouncement of almost certain death—becomes an inner quest beyond sorrows toward a universal core. Like all life's passages—through adolescence, through the middle years, through menopause—this passage is one of discovery.

From the beginning of my illness, I ached to communicate to my three-year-old daughter, Emmy. Emmy had come into our lives at two months of age. When we adopted her, we were offering the promise of a stable home and intact family. Now, that seemed threatened. In becoming sick, I felt I had cheated her.

After I was diagnosed, I began to write letters to her, imagining that she would read them when she was grown. Often I wrote with a throbbing head, on painkillers, so weak that I had difficulty remembering what had happened hours before. But I forced myself.

In these letters, I grappled with inchoate emotions I had a hard time articulating, even to my wife. Each letter forced me to confront some fundamental element of the human condition: love, fear, sorrow, joy, marriage, parenthood, death.

These were postcards from a storm. The letters described this final passage *as I lived it,* recording what I saw, felt, and thought in the midst of this turmoil, not in retrospect. They never sanitized my sorrow and fear.

Eventually, editors at a Virginia newspaper encouraged me to write a first-person account including material from these letters. When the articles ran in February 1993, I feared being ridiculed for being frank and unashamedly sentimental. Instead, within hours I began to receive hundreds of phone calls and letters. I talked to countless strangers, sometimes for hours, who said that I had told *their* stories.

A man with multiple sclerosis said the articles made him feel less alone. A woman diagnosed as clinically depressed said she found consolation and strength in how I grappled with my sorrow.

A cancer patient who had trouble articulating his turmoil gave the articles to his wife and told her, "This is what I've been trying to tell you."

The emotions were universal even if the diseases and challenges were different.

I heard from oncologists, family practitioners, and medical specialists whose careers involved treating critically ill patients. In most cases, they said the articles offered them a rare glimpse— from the patient's point of view—of the range of emotions caused by serious, especially terminal, illnesses. Doctors had prescribed brain scans and blood tests without ever recognizing the pain and discomfort so many of them cause. One doctor said he read my account of going through a multiple resonance imaging scanner (MRI) as if it were a work of science fiction. A family practitioner in Washington distributed copies to all the physicians in his practice, hoping it would help them practice better medicine.

I heard from many people who were perfectly healthy. Reading about this struggle helped free them from the paralysis created by our culture's code of silence surrounding serious illness and death. They wanted to talk about something they'd avoided even thinking about before. In contemplating death, many found, one rediscovers life.

When I wrote the letters excerpted here, I had no notion of publishing them as a book. They were my private communications, recording my love for my daughter. In retrospect, they read much like a journal a father might keep recording his toddler's growth. Despite all the pain, fear, frustration, and remaining uncertainty, however, I see this journal recording a time when both of us grew.

MAGIC AND LOSS

Dear Emmy,

About two weeks ago I suffered a seizure and headed to DePaul Hospital nearby, where doctors discovered I had a brain tumor.

A neurosurgeon checked me into DePaul and removed the tumor. He believes it's benign. But he, and others, made it clear the tumor will most likely grow back. Maybe in six months, maybe in one year, maybe in ten—but at *some* point—it will probably kill me.

I write these letters now filled with sorrow that I may never see you graduate from high school or college; that I may not be able to watch you grow up, have children and start your own family. The thought saddens me because that's what I've always wanted. To see my sweet baby daughter blossom into a young woman, a world traveler, an adventurer.

At times, fear and sorrow overwhelm me. Other times, confidence overwhelms me. I picture you and me 20 years from now huddling together, reading from these letters and laughing. Still, I write these letters with the understanding that that may never happen. These letters I write to you, Emmy, so you'll never forget your daddy and his undying love.

Sunday, May 24

Dear Emmy,

Today as I lie in my hospital bed, my head throbs and a scar shoots pain deep into my skull.

I lie alone now in a pleasant pinkish room. A hospital room. A television is mounted on one wall. Books are stacked on my end table. Balloons and get-well cards are scattered here and there. The phone rings probably 20 times a day. I often find myself chatting with college buddies or childhood friends. I've come to know nurses and orderlies and nuns at DePaul Hospital. But when orderlies leave and the phone stops ringing, I lie bored, restless.

I've never spent much time in a hospital. In my 37 years, I've always been healthy. I've taken probably ten sick days from work in my life. In the hospital, everything seems perfectly controlled. There are no hot days, no cold days, no sunny days, no windy days. The sun never sets in here or rises in the morning.

I can see some grass and trees out a narrow window, but I'm inside, cordoned off, inside this *perfect* world, the hospital world, this world that has me longing for nature's imperfections.

I'm here because I am sick. Because I am dying. I'm frightened but most people don't want to hear about my fears. Fear builds walls between people. Many people express sympathy by telling me stories about people they've *known* who were sick.

Today, I'm supposed to be recuperating, reading books, relaxing. But I can't read. I pick up a book and stare at the pages. My eyes ache. My mind drifts to the thousands of images of the last two weeks. The reality that only two weeks have passed startles me.

Emmy, my lovely little girl, I feel this urge to talk to you, to tell you what I'm feeling. But that's impossible. You're just a baby, only three years old. You live in a world of crayons and swings and sandboxes. Even if we could sit down to talk, how could I explain in words you'd understand? How do you explain tumors and illness and death to a three-year-old? So I write down my thoughts for the day you wonder, "What ever happened to Daddy?"

I have a hard time summarizing the last two weeks, because there's been so much and I recall so little. What I do remember vividly is the life that Mommy and I lived before the tumor.

Emmy, I want you to know, your mommy and I always loved each other. That may sound corny. In those first days we met, I guess I thought that love was just a conglomeration of other emotions—respect, companionship, trust. But there's more, Emmy. Something beyond that.

For Mommy and me, companionship goes back 16 years to a night we met at the Catalyst, a bar and restaurant in Santa Cruz, California. Mommy came to the Catalyst to dance. She later said she was attracted to me by my black hair and my Converse high-top sneakers. She asked me to dance.

That first night, we spent hours talking about travel, adventure, life, values, love, friendship. I've always been shy around women, but I clearly remember leaning over and kissing your mommy, gently, on the cheek.

Ten days after we met, we started to live out adventures we talked about that first night.

We drove to the Mexican border. For breakfast one morning, we went to a back-street cafe in Obregon, a cafe with two wobbly formica tables. We sat down and ate scrambled eggs spiced with Chorizo. Another time, we stood for an hour in a warm summer downpour waiting for a bus. When the bus arrived, all the seats were full. The driver let us sit on an ice chest next to him. We sat side-by-side on the ice chest, leaning on the dash, listening to the slap of the windshield wipers, gazing at the rain-soaked countryside, watching a glorious orange Mexican sunset.

What I remember most, though, was when we rode through Mexico's Sonora desert aboard a slow-moving train with wood-slat seats. The train was filthy. Dust blew in the open windows. At the train stations, street hawkers peddled potatoes wrapped in flour tortillas. We reached out, bought them, and ate them with everybody else.

On one leg of that journey, an old woman and old man sat across from us. The woman reclined a bit in her seat and the old man—probably 80 years old—stood next to her, holding her shoulder.

This old couple looked so loving. The train was full of empty seats, but the old man insisted on standing there, leaning over, holding this woman's shoulder.

When we got married three years later, Mommy had my wedding band engraved with these initials: FLTOC. Forever Like The Old Couple.

Mommy and I, from those earliest days, were *companeros*. Love sucked oxygen from each adventure—from the rain and the dust and even the sense of being lost in a faraway land.

We were so young, so *alive*. In years since, love, travel, and adventure seemed intertwined. We spent one summer in Paris studying French. After I graduated from Berkeley, Mommy and I spent a year in Jamaica and a year in Ecuador.

I have sweet memories of the streets of Mandeville, Jamaica, of walking into the hamlet of El Carmen, Ecuador, to see horses tied to hitches downtown.

After returning from South America, I began writing for newspapers. After years of hard work, Mommy earned her doctorate. Seven years ago, a Virginia university hired Mommy and I got a job at the newspaper here.

But we never forgot how much we loved to travel. During springs and summers, we toured Europe, sleeping on trains, carrying nothing more than day packs for three-week jaunts. We flew to Istanbul, Turkey, awoke to the haunting sounds of chant-ing from mosques, wandered through the ancient Grand Bazaar.

We never intended to stay in Virginia for more than two years. But Mommy got tenure. We bought a home. We made friends. We established roots.

We wanted someone else to share our love and our adventures. When Mommy couldn't conceive a baby, we decided to adopt. Somehow, it seemed *right*. It seemed fated.

That's how you came into our lives. I remember those first moments holding you, Emmy. You were two months old. Even at two months, you were spunky. You looked right at me with a goofy, toothless smile. At that moment, I felt love in its purest form, love stripped of adventure, of history. I didn't *learn* to love you, Emmy. Love was just *there*, deep in my guts. I was your *daddy*.

Since then, Mommy's worked as a professor at the university. She's had long holidays and summers off. At the newspaper, I often worked longer hours than I wanted. Some nights I didn't get home until you were asleep. Some weeks I'd see you only in the mornings.

We still had adventures. When you were 21 months old, we spent several weeks in Wales. Mommy and I would often dream of what we'd do in our future. Mommy was always talking about coming up with a "five year plan," some idea of what we'd like to be doing five years from now. We talked about living in Greece, or in the Caribbean. We talked about spending a year in Africa. Someday, Mommy wanted to travel around the world. More immediately, Mommy wanted to take a year off to teach in the Czech Republic. These were dreams that hung before us.

Then in May it all went wrong. My recollections of what happened are garbled. I remember reading you a story, putting you to bed, then falling asleep. There was nothing unusual about that night—until a smoke alarm rang out at three o'clock in the morning.

Mommy and I, both dead asleep, awoke panicked, fearing there was a fire. In the darkness, I scrambled out of bed, afraid we would be trapped. My heart pounded.

As it turned out, the smoke detector rang out because batteries were going bad. I pulled out the batteries and climbed back into bed. I remember what a struggle it was to calm myself. My heart hammered, making my head throb.

Eventually, I guess, I fell asleep. Most of the rest of that night I learned about from Mommy. Before daybreak, I started to thrash.

"Stop that," Mommy told me. "That isn't funny."

But I kept thrashing.

"Stop that," she shouted. "You're scaring me."

The thrashing got worse. It dawned on Mommy that I was having a seizure. I was incoherent, flailing my arms and my legs. You got out of bed to see your daddy convulsing. Mommy asked you to move away.

Mommy phoned for an ambulance. When paramedics got to our house, I seemed to slip in and out of consciousness. I once sat on the edge of our bed, my eyes dilated, staring at a wall.

"Please," I pleaded in a frightened tone. *"Please."* Mommy was heartbroken. She thought her friend, her lover, her *companero,* was dying.

Slowly I seemed to emerge from the seizures. Paramedics allowed me walk to our bathroom. In the bathroom, convulsions hit again. I collapsed onto the bathroom's tile floor with so much force that the impact fractured one of the vertebrae in my back. Paramedics strapped me onto a gurney and took me to an ambulance.

This is where I had my first, foggy memory. Emerging from a haze I saw you, Emmy. You stood in the ambulance, next to me. You were wearing your pink terry cloth robe. Your "housecoat" you always called it. You'd always loved that robe. Now you looked so frightened.

I have vague recollections of people milling outside the ambulance. I reached out. I had no idea what had happened. I wanted so much to touch you and Mommy.

My memory fades out. My next clear recollection is lying in bed in DePaul Hospital. I was in the emergency room, in a hospital bed, surrounded by a white curtain. There was an opening in the curtain that allowed me to see doctors and nurses milling around.

Then I saw you. You still wore the pink robe. You stood in a towering white hospital corridor. You looked so dainty, so helpless. I noticed your root-beer brown eyes. Such beautiful eyes. But those eyes looked so sad. You stood staring at your daddy strapped into a hospital bed with needles in his arms. I ached to erase your fear and sadness. I ached to hold you. But I couldn't.

As I became more aware, I complained about my back. A doctor decided to get an x-ray. A neurosurgeon, Dr. Jonathan Partington, ordered a CAT scan. A CAT scan is a type of brain x-ray that allows doctors to see inside your head. Partington believed the CAT scan might find out what caused the seizures.

You and Mommy went home to change clothes. The chronology still confuses me. But I remember the pain of my back as I lay down on a hard, narrow table for the CAT scan.

"Don't move," a tinny, disembodied voice ordered over a speaker in the scanner. I lay motionless, still aching, struggling to keep my eyes from blurring. I listened to the CAT scan churn. Throughout, I figured this was routine. No big deal. Doctors *always* ran tests.

After half an hour nurses put me back on the gurney and pushed me to the emergency room. Later, someone said I needed an MRI, too. The MRI is an newer, much more precise brain scan.

Nobody told me why I needed an MRI. I guess this started to worry me a bit. But then I thought—why worry? If they wanted to get a better look at my brain, why not?

The MRI room was freezing. Technicians said the MRI scanner needed coolers to keep its magnets from overheating. All dressed in white, they struggled to get me onto the table without tearing up my back. That proved impossible. I shouted out in pain as they moved me onto another hard, narrow table.

My head rested in a plastic cradle to keep me perfectly still. They put on a kind of plastic mask with a mirror, inches above my eyes, tilted at a 45-degree angle.

"Are you claustrophobic?" a woman asked.

"No," I answered. Then they eased my body deep into the MRI's throat, a tube so narrow that my arms pushed against my sides.

"This scan will last about eight minutes," said a metallic voice from a speaker above my head. The scanner emitted hydraulic creaks, as if calibrating itself. Then the jackhammer-clanging began. The scanner sounded broken, as if its motors were about to explode. The sound, this awful, deafening growl, didn't stop through the entire scan. When the sound did stop, the silence came so suddenly it almost startled me.

"This next scan is going to last about six minutes," the metallic voice announced. Then the growling and banging began again.

After several scans, they pulled me from the machine's throat. "See anything in there?" I asked the woman who had been standing at the console.

"The radiologist has to read it," the woman said without a trace of emotion, as if stating an obvious rule.

Nurses wheeled me back to the emergency room. They pulled the curtain around my bed. At last, I was allowed to lie alone. I lay in my cubicle, unable to see anything but the needles in my arm, the plastic medicine bag hanging over me, the curtains around me.

Still, I couldn't sleep. In the bed next to me I heard moaning and vomiting. It started to make me feel sick.

"I'll never overdose again," I heard a man tell a nurse as the retching stopped. He sounded young. I thought over and over about what he'd said. "I'll never overdose again." Somehow, as I lay in the bed, his words haunted me. "I'll never overdose again." It stuck in my mind. What had he overdosed on? Cocaine?

Heroin? Crack? I had no idea. After what seemed hours, he got up to leave, and I could make him out through the crack in the curtain. He was young, blond, probably 22 years old, wearing baggy shorts and a T-shirt.

All this struck me as strange. Maybe he had been at a friend's house, taking whatever it is he overdosed on. Suddenly, somebody must have noticed that he was out of control. And he ends up, on the other side of the curtain, vomiting, surrounded by nurses and doctors, suffering his own nightmarish agonies.

People never *plan* to go to the emergency room. That's the whole idea of having an emergency room—for *emergencies*. You end up in a room with people who have nothing in common but some sudden, unplanned medical trauma. The emergency room exists for the day fate intrudes. Fate brought us into the same room, but we'd probably never see each other again. He'd go back to his friends. And I. . .well, where would I end up?

A few beds away, another lady bellowed, *"Let me go!"* The woman's voice was labored. She slurred syllables, making everything sound unhinged. "Let me go!" she shouted again. "I *demand* that you let me go *right now*." Her words carried a sense of confusion and derangement. I don't know why, but her shouting frightened me. "LET ME GO!" she shouted and I could hear scuffling. Her voice seemed to be moving around the emergency room. Someone told her they'd called her doctor, a psychiatrist, I assumed. But she continued shouting. "I DEMAND THAT YOU LET ME GO. I DEMAND TO SEE A LAWYER." I lay in bed, bombarded by the sounds of the emergency room, waiting for you and Mommy to come back. I too, had become a kind of inmate of this hospital world, cordoned behind this curtain, lying in a bed with chrome bars, confined by needles and monitors hooked to my body, Finally, I drifted off.

Mommy returned in an hour without you. She sat on a chair to my right. About daybreak, Dr. Partington came to my bed. He opened the curtain and introduced himself. He seemed articulate. Reassuring. He wore gray tortoise-shell glasses that slid down his nose a bit. He hung up one of the MRI films. He told us, very succinctly, with no alarm, that I had a tumor, a "common" brain tumor. I remember the comfort I took in that word, *common. Rare,* for me, was a spookier word.

The tumor, Partington told us, was probably an astrocytoma. He told us the kind of cells that made up the tumor. He told us the shape of the cells. He told us everything a doctor should tell a patient. Probably more. Mommy and I acted calm and asked questions. To the surgeon, I'm sure we seemed to be taking it all in. I suppose we were. But all his explanations, all his talk about "astrocytes" and possible "oligodendroglioma," got swallowed up in *one* word.

Tumor.

Tumor. A strange sounding word, a word that can create instant dread. To have a tumor is to. . .what? I didn't even know. I didn't even really know what a tumor was. It was a demon whose face I'd never seen, whose shape I'd never taken the trouble to imagine. Still, in life, the demon was always there, always lurking in the shadows. People worry about "tumors" without even knowing what they're worrying about.

I had a brain tumor. I could *see* it on the piece of film hanging before me. The MRI film was almost beautiful, so vivid, so finely etched, showing the structure and the folds of my brain. But the tumor showed no detail. It was probably the size of an egg, maybe larger, white and featureless, inside my skull.

Dr. Partington said it appeared benign. For Mommy and me, that was a word that stuck. I could feel my guts unwind.

Benign. That was another word that carried emotional impact, even when we don't know the meaning. I knew it was the *good* word, the one you wanted tagged to the word, *tumor.* It meant that the tumor wasn't *malignant,* a word that carried such frightening connotations.

Still, what did *benign* really mean? Partington talked about it somewhat, but, again, it all escaped me. I had a tumor. It was benign. That was all I seemed to retain.

"What do we do now?" I asked.

The doctor said I had to be checked into the intensive care ward. He'd give me anti-convulsants and steroids to cut down on the swelling in my brain. Then, in several days, he'd cut open my scalp, saw out a chunk of my skull, and carve out the tumor. To be safe, he said, he'd have to slice out some healthy brain, too.

Partington said there were risks to the surgery. I could lose some function in my right side or suffer problems with my speech. But the tumor had to come out. If he didn't take it out, it would kill me.

After he left, Mommy and I had so many questions. But nothing articulate. They weren't even questions, really. They were explosions of fear and confusion. We struggled to soak in what had been told to us. To soak in a cordial chat that suddenly, irrevocably, altered our lives. It was like being sucked into a raging river.

After a couple days in intensive care, I moved into a large, pleasant room in the regular hospital. Doctors said it would take several days for the brain swelling to decrease enough to undergo surgery.

Before surgery, I had a lot of visitors. My mother, your grandma, flew in from California. Some friends came from work.

I told everyone the same story. The tumor was benign. I'd survive. No need to worry. Mommy and I had talked ourselves into accepting the reality of a few days in the hospital, a few months of recovery.

I still remember the morning of surgery. They put me on a surgical bed. I kissed Mommy. They wheeled me toward some kind of pre-op room.

Now, *that* was a strange feeling—lying flat on my back, looking up at the ceiling, at the light fixtures, barely making out doctors and nurses passing in the corridors, white and green phantoms in my peripheral vision.

I couldn't see the rooms or other patients or even the other beds. In the pre-op room a man in green scrubs stood next to my bed talking about the anesthesia. I felt the hard puncture as he slid a fat needle into my arm. He said a few words. . .

For the next six hours, Mommy and Grandma sat in a waiting room, scared to death. They waited, worried, cried. But for me, it was instantaneous. One moment they were wheeling me to surgery. The next moment, I was in the intensive care unit, looking up at IV lines, curtains, and heart monitors, breathing through a bulky plastic oxygen mask, watching Mommy coming toward me in tears.

Mommy grabbed my hand.

"It's *benign!*" she said through the tears. "It's *benign!*" I slowly kicked my legs and waved my arms. My mouth was dried out from the anesthesia. Mommy gave me ice chips. "I can *move,*" I said, stretching out my words. I asked Mommy to kiss me. She pecked my cheek. "No," I said through my oxygen mask, "a French kiss."

After I got out of intensive care and got my bandages off, I saw my head. Dr. Partington hadn't touched my beard, but he shaved the front half of my hair. In the back, my hair still hung over my hospital gown. The scar over the top of my head was jagged, running almost ear to ear. There were dents where Dr. Partington drilled through my skull. As I looked in the mirror I felt nausea.

Friends visited soon after I had the bandages removed. I could see them staring at the scar and the shaved portion of my head. After they left, Mommy cut the rest of my hair short to make the contrast less startling. She found a blue cloth surgical cap that I wore when visitors came.

With the cap on, I looked normal again. I tried to put everything into perspective: the scar, the lumps and the shaved head shouldn't really bother me that much. My hair would grow back.

A couple of days later, Mommy and Grandma were sitting in my hospital room when Dr. Partington showed up. He must have come from another operation. I see him clearly, leaning against the wall beyond the foot of my bed, wearing scrubs, looking tired, eating an ice cream bar. I wondered what kind of operation he'd just performed. Who was the patient? Was the operation a success?

In a relaxed tone, Partington said DePaul's pathologist, the doctor who examined cells to determine the nature of diseases, had examined parts of my tumor removed during surgery. The pathologist, Partington said, thought part of my tumor was "anaplastic."

I didn't know what *anaplastic* meant, precisely, but I knew it meant, basically, that the tumor was malignant. As Partington spoke, I felt blood course through my body.

I had a hard time asking questions or even catching my breath. He was so *calm*, so relaxed. Somehow, that confused me. Mommy stood up next to my bed and took my hand.

Partington said he wasn't sure he agreed with the diagnosis of the hospital pathologist. Partington had seen the tumor during surgery and it didn't appear malignant to him. This confused me. Two doctors, two specialists, people who presumably know as much as anyone about tumors and cancers, disagreed about something so fundamental. One thought my tumor was benign. The other thought it was malignant. How could that happen?

Partington, still calm, still relaxed, explained how difficult it can be to make judgments on pathology. Doctors had no trouble identifying clearly benign cells, or clearly malignant cells, but between the two was a gray area, an area where doctors had to make judgments based on slices of the tumor placed on glass and stained with various chemicals. As he spoke, I realized I had almost no notion of the medical meaning of those words—*benign* and *malignant*.

Mommy and Grandma and I listened dumbfoundedly. Suddenly, this stuff about "benign" and "malignant" seemed more complicated. Not even *doctors* could agree.

Partington told us he'd mailed the slides of the tumor to the Armed Forces Institute of Pathology in Washington, D.C., to be examined by neuropathologists, specialists in brain tissue cells.

The AFIP was the "gold standard" of diagnosis, he said. "The best."

When Partington left, I felt as if I were falling, unable to control anything. This meant. . .suffering, and death. Just a few days before, I thought about going back to work, about getting back to my "life." Now all that seemed so *petty*.

Sorrow exploded within me so powerfully that it seemed part of my body, like an arm or a leg. It was there, undeniably there, overwhelming everything else. I didn't feel just for myself. I felt guilty. I felt as if I'd betrayed you, and Mommy, and Grandma. As Mommy cried, I felt bad for inflicting pain on this woman who shared my life and my adventures. Am I going to leave her a widow? How could I do this to her? Or to you, my beautiful baby girl? How could I leave you without a daddy?

Grandma tried to be upbeat. She didn't believe this stuff about the tumor being malignant. In her gut, she *knew* it *wasn't* malignant. After all, Dr. Partington didn't *agree* that the tumor was malignant. He was the surgeon. Everything was going to be okay. There was no reason to cry.

But I thought about my sisters, Kay, Karen, Gail. About my brother, Doug. About my dad. I worried about suffering. Suffering scares me. Even more, I worried about you *watching* me suffer. I worried about Mommy, in the hospital, having to make a decision to let me die.

I feel compelled to keep all of you from suffering. But there seems only one way: to *live*. Now that seems beyond my control.

That's all in other people's hands.

Dear Emmy,

Today one of Dr. Partington's associates came in and asked if I felt any pain. When I said I felt fine, he said I was free to leave the hospital. He wrote out prescriptions for anti-seizure drugs and painkillers.

There were some restrictions. I can't drive for at least six months because of the possibility that I could have another seizure. "You can chase your wife around if you want," the doctor told me, "and if she lets you catch her that's fine too."

Soon after, a medical technician showed up to fit me with an aluminum-and-leather back brace. Although I'd been anxious to leave, my discharge seemed so sudden, so unexpected. After I got my back brace, I phoned Mommy and asked her to come pick me up. Within half an hour, Mommy was there packing everything in my room—all the cards, books, letters, balloons, and flowers. And hats. A lot of people gave me hats to cover up my shaved and scarred head. I put on a hat and eased into a wheelchair.

Since we had so many balloons I decided to give one to Grace, a patient I'd met in the hospital. Grace had a brain tumor removed five years ago. The tumor had been benign. Then a month ago, Grace began to have pounding headaches. Doctors found that the tumor had come back, swollen to the size of an orange.

With a tumor that large, nobody could say she'd come out of surgery without being crippled. Her surgery was just before mine. I remember because they bumped up her surgery time, making it early in the morning. Her dad, who didn't know about the time change, was driving up from North Carolina and would be too late to wish her luck. She was frightened about going into surgery with no friends or family around.

Grace came through surgery better than anyone expected. Her speech was fine and she didn't have any paralysis. A few times, after my surgery, she'd come into my room.

"I'm *so* lucky," she told me.

As we left the hospital, Mommy wheeled me by Grace's room. The room was dark. I could see Grace on her side curled in her bed. As we came to the door, she heard us and rolled over, drugged and groggy.

"I'm leaving today," I told her.

"*Oh*," she said, stretching out the word a bit. Mommy tied the balloon to her bed.

"Good luck," I said. I left her room aware I'd never see Grace again; I'd never know how her life turned out.

When we got to the main floor of the hospital we walked by other patients, nurses, doctors, administrators. I was low in the wheelchair, wearing my ball cap and my back brace, looking up at them. Nobody looked directly at me. They averted their eyes, as if my illness were causing *them* discomfort and embarrassment.

When Mommy wheeled me out of the hospital I was blasted by warm, humid air. Mommy went to get the car and I sat looking at trees and cars and grass and sky. I could feel the sun, hot on my arms, and smell the fresh cut grass. Mommy pulled the car around and helped me ease into the front seat wearing my back brace.

I remember pulling up to our house, looking at everything with fresh eyes—our trees, our fence, our bushes, our porch. Mommy parked and I hobbled toward the house. When she opened the front door, I looked around overwhelmed. The dark hardwood floors shone. On the walls were photographs of our adventures. Over the couch was an oil painting from Haiti next to a *mola* from Panama. I looked at our antique oak dining room table and the carpet we bought in Pamukale, Turkey.

Everything was familiar yet every room seemed fresh. Laid before me were the mementos of my lifetime.

"It's *so* beautiful," I said. "I can't believe it. Everything is so *beautiful.*"

In the dining room were more balloons and more cards and flowers. In the kitchen were trays of food brought over by neighbors and friends.

Mommy left to get medicine and to pick you up from day camp. I lay propped on the couch, leafing through the mail, talking to Grandma.

When you came back, Emmy, you ran in the door, shouting, "Daddy! Daddy!" You were gentle. You didn't jump on the couch or jerk me. You kissed my cheek and snuggled into my arm. Your daddy was home. You just wanted to be near me. Our family was back together, in our home.

Tuesday, May 26

Dear Emmy,

Grandma flew back to California today.

This ordeal has been rough on Grandma, too. Two of my uncles—her brothers—recently died of cancer. At our home, Grandma couldn't sleep.

I wanted to go to the airport, but Mommy thought it would hurt my back. She was probably right. But she also thought I was too sick to leave alone. So after I said goodbye to Grandma, a neighbor came to the house to make sure I was okay.

The neighbor, Bill, has always been friendly. His wife had taken Grandma around. They always offered to pitch in. Before I came home, Bill mowed our lawn.

As you, Grandma and Mommy left, I settled on the couch. Bill and I talked about politics, news, books, and magazines. Still, somehow it struck me that he was there in part to babysit. Just *in case* something happened. It disturbed me, made me feel so feeble, so helpless.

After you and Mommy got home from the airport, Bill left and the three of us spent a quiet evening together.

Mommy told me you've been having a tough time, too. Once, when Grandma said she didn't feel well, you asked, "Are you going to fall down and shake like daddy?" During my first days in the hospital, you were too frightened to sleep in your room. You slept with Mommy, holding her hand.

Mommy needed to do something to take your mind off hospitals and illness. She signed you up for a "summer day camp" at the Jewish Community Center. You went to the JCC every day to swim, dance, and do gymnastics. Mommy arranged to have you visit friends' homes. But you still missed your daddy. You continued to be haunted by nightmares. You started to wet your bed at night, something you haven't done for more than a year.

Now that I was home, you wanted my company. Today we lay on my bed watching a cartoon Mommy rented for us. At bedtime, you asked me to read you a story.

Tonight that was hard. My back was cramping. I was totally exhausted. Still, those moments were precious as we lay together and I read you a story about Elmer, the patchwork elephant.

Dear Emmy,

Today our lives seemed to get back to a more regular pattern. In the morning, Mommy took you to camp. She headed to the university where she had to catch up on work. I convinced her it was okay to leave me alone in our home.

Soon after she left, I got a call from Dr. Partington's office. The doctor wanted to see us in his office at 11:30 that morning. I called Mommy at work. She canceled her meetings. She rushed. We went to Partington's office, anxious about being summoned so suddenly.

At the doctor's office we were escorted into a small medical examination room with a chair, a stool, and an examining table covered with paper. Mommy and I sat alone wondering what Partington wanted to tell us. I could hear Partington's muffled voice in another examination room. I wondered: How can anyone deliver so much bad news?

You're going to die.

You're never going to walk again.

In the other room, Partington's voice trailed off.

He opened the door and stepped into our room seeming relaxed and happy.

"I figured you'd want to know as soon as I got word," Partington said as he leaned on the examination table. He told us he'd gotten a preliminary pathology report from the Armed Forces Institute of Pathology. Doctors there determined that my tumor was, in fact, benign.

"That's great," I said.

Mommy was pleased, too. She's been so worried. Now it

seemed our worries were ending. I had a tumor. Dr. Partington removed it. It was benign. End of story. Time to get better.

Then Dr. Partington suggested I make an appointment for radiation treatment. Partington said he had consulted two of the nation's top experts in brain tumor research, one at Yale, another in San Francisco. He telephoned them to get suggestions about further treatment in my case.

The Yale doctor suggested that I forego radiation treatment altogether—because radiation therapy didn't seem to make any difference in survival or recurrence. The San Francisco doctor suggested I begin radiation therapy immediately. Partington recommended that I take radiation treatments.

"But I thought it was *benign*," Mommy said.

"It *is*," Dr. Partington said. "But these tend to come back." If he left anything behind, even one cell, it would return. The radiation could destroy lingering cells.

Not even radiation would guarantee a cure, he said. Radiation was unlikely to destroy all the cells but it would probably delay recurrence.

Mommy seemed confused by all this. Radiation for a benign tumor wasn't something either of us had considered. Everything Dr. Partington told us had a familiar ring. I'm sure we'd heard it all before, but now. . .now it seemed to come out of the blue. A benign tumor that kills. Lingering cells.

Mommy asked Partington about rates of survival for benign astrocytomas. I don't think we'd ever gotten this specific before. Dr. Partington seemed reluctant to answer. Mommy pushed.

With benign astrocytomas, he said almost apologetically, patients have roughly a 20-percent chance of surviving five to 10 years. I don't remember his exact words. I remember only that we were destroyed.

Twenty percent.

Partington went on to explain that I had a lot going for me. The tumor was removed. I came out of surgery without apparent impairments. I was relatively young. There was new technology, like the MRI, to catch recurring tumors early. There was promising research in radiation, in chemotherapy, and especially in biological and genetic medicine. Soon enough, there might be a cure.

Still, he said, the tumors tend to return. Nobody knew when that would happen in my case. If I could make it two years without any recurrence, my chances would improve a lot.

Twenty percent.

Two years.

I was too busy comforting Mommy to listen well.

We walked out of the examination room into the waiting room. We sat waiting to fill out paperwork, waiting to make an appointment with a radiation specialist.

While we waited, Mommy leaned forward, placing her head in her hands. She stared blankly and then, suddenly, it all seemed to wash over her. Her face contorted as she tried to hold back tears. She couldn't.

While I took care of the paperwork, Mommy sat and sobbed.

Sunday, May 30

Dear Emmy,

This weekend, Mommy and I went to the Eastern Virginia Medical School library. After talking to Dr. Partington, I had a sense that I wanted to know more. I wanted to know if there were treatments he hadn't considered. I wanted to know, precisely, what was inside my brain. In gathering information, I reasoned, I could gather power.

Mommy didn't want me to go to the library because I still was weak. But I insisted. I decided I'd handle my medical case like I'd handled stories as a reporter.

I walked into the library wearing my back brace and my hat, carrying a blank legal pad and several pens. At the library, I hooked into a computerized data base of medical journals. I searched for any article that mentioned my condition and came across more than 200 citations over the last three years. I printed out the list and circled promising titles. I gave Mommy the call numbers and she went to the shelves and pulled the journals.

Before I copied anything, I scanned the articles. Most were technical, with titles like "Low-Grade Astrocytomas: Treatment with Unconventionally Fractionated External Beam Stereotactic Radiation Therapy." Somehow, this seemed a mission. Somewhere in this mass of incomprehensible jargon I would find the *answer*. And I would live.

I looked at the graphs accompanying these articles, graphs representing "survival." The graphs were traditional, with a vertical bar representing the percentage of patients and a horizontal bar representing time.

The line sloping down from that vertical bar meant patients

were dying. When the line sloped all the way to the horizontal bar it meant the patients, every single one, had died.

As I looked at these graphs, I felt sick. All the lines sloped down. Gracefully but irrevocably. There didn't seem to be an escape. Sometimes, lives were measured in years. More often, lives were measured in months.

Some articles examined different treatments: radiation, chemotherapy, surgery. The articles arguing against radiation for benign tumors simply made the point that radiation didn't seem to make much difference in the survival curve. Another article pointed out that people who went through intensive brain radiation survived longer—but sometimes ended up so neurologically damaged that they were unable to work or take care of themselves. Some ended up living in nursing homes.

With or without radiation, people died. Almost inevitably. There was a handful of "long-term" survivors, but they were treated as aberrations.

I also looked up articles on malignant tumors. Mommy didn't want to see those articles. They depressed her. The lines sloped in the same fashion. But life was sometimes measured in *weeks* not months. Dr. Partington had told us the names of the neurosurgeons he consulted, so I did a computer search of the articles they'd written, too.

When I got home, I phoned the doctor at Yale, the one who had argued that radiation therapy didn't seem to increase survival in cases of low-grade or benign tumors.

I called everywhere. I phoned the National Brain Tumor Association. I phoned a similar association in Canada. I phoned one of my uncles, a doctor now suffering from cancer of the liver. But I found nothing. I became familiar with the vocabulary. But that vocabulary all boiled down to the same thing.

Astrocytomas kill.

Dear Emmy,

Radiation.

I don't even like saying the word.

This morning, I talked to my mother. I told her the tumor appeared benign. She seemed relieved. I mentioned that the doctor had recommended radiation. She seemed stunned.

If it's a benign tumor, she wanted to know, why radiation? I explained about the chance that some cells might be left behind.

So radiation would take care of it, once and for all?

No. . .I explained the stuff I didn't want to think about. I told her about the study showing that radiation didn't make all that much difference in survival. My mother, I knew, had been taking everything hard. My sisters said she sometimes cried herself to sleep. I didn't want to make things worse.

I heard from friends, too, and went through the same questions and answers, trying to sound upbeat. The more I talked, the more I seemed to be talking myself out of radiation. Why undergo the very real potential complications of radiation if I wouldn't live any longer?

Mommy and I started to doubt everything we'd heard and read. So much of it was contradictory. I'd fish around for the most optimistic articles, but even they frightened me. I had no idea how to sort it all. Then, moments later, I'd find myself feeling hopeful. Mommy and I would rehash everything. We talked about every sentence, every phrase, every nuance. We talked about new treatments using radiation, chemotherapy, genetically engineered viruses, or extract of shark cartilage. Researchers were moving fast. If I could make it five years, they'd have a cure, I figured. That was the key. Not to live forever, just to live for the cure.

I'd get another phone call, or another visit from an old friend or someone from work. I would explain everything again. In quiet moments, though, it would hit me.

This tumor is going to kill me.

I'm dying.

That was the issue. This wasn't about cancer, brain tumors, radiation. This was about facing mortality. I could have been diagnosed with AIDS, or dozens of other terminal illnesses. Death is death. All this chatter about my tumor, about the cells, about the treatments, was just that, chatter, giving us something to talk about without mentioning the word *death*.

I'm dying.

No, I'm not dying, I'd tell myself.

Yet nobody seemed to be able to settle the issue for me.

My doctor recommended a group of radiation specialists at DePaul Hospital Cancer Center. Feeling confused about everything, Mommy and I walked through the same hospital corridors we'd walked a few days before, past the gift and balloon shop, past the chapel.

In the waiting room of the radiation specialist's office I looked around at the other patients. An older man sat across from me with a big red square and a small x drawn on his neck in India ink. To one side was a skinny guy, who looked exhausted, next to a heavyset woman.

"It's going to be okay," Mommy whispered as she held my hand.

A few moments after we walked in, nurses led us to the doctor's examining room. It was like all the others with a chair and an examination table. I sat on the table and listened to the paper crackle beneath me.

One of the radiation specialists came in, introduced himself as Dr. Sinesi, and sat at a metal desk. As he did, he looked over my chart. Dr. Sinesi talked to us as if radiation were *inevitable*. Mommy asked whether there would be side effects.

"Probably not much," he said, "other than hair loss."

"Will it grow back?" Mommy asked.

"No," he said. "I'm afraid not. It will probably be permanent."

Dr. Sinesi started to talk about starting treatments. At this point, Mommy and I made it clear we hadn't decided that we were going through with radiation therapy. Sinesi seemed surprised.

Sinesi acknowledged that intensive radiation therapy to the brain could be performed only once without causing potentially catastrophic brain damage. I talked about Partington's ability to monitor my tumor with frequent MRI exams.

"If it comes back, he can go in, cut out the regrowth and I could begin radiation at that point," I said. "If that's a couple years down the line I might buy a couple years."

"But this condition is *curable*," Dr. Sinesi said.

I'd learned that "curable" meant only that the patient survived five years without recurrence. In the case of benign astrocytomas, some patients made it seven years, even eight years. Then the tumors came back. They are cured. Then they die.

"What do you mean by curable?" I asked.

"Five years," Sinesi said.

Five years. What is five years? In five years, Emmy, you'll be just eight years old.

Sinesi agreed that delaying radiation was a *possibility*. It was my choice. He looked at the report by the DePaul pathologist. He said if I truly had anaplastic cells in the tumor, he'd have to push for radiation.

I told him about the AFIP report we'd gotten from Partington revealing that the tumor was benign. As we talked to Dr. Sinesi, Mommy and I decided to get a third pathology report, just to confirm that I didn't, in fact, have a malignant tumor.

Sinesi called Partington and gave me the phone. I asked Partington if he could arrange to have another pathologist examine the slides of my tumor.

"This is a big decision," I told him.

Partington agreed to another neuropathologist's opinion but said delaying radiation could be risky. Besides, he'd finally gotten in the final report from the AFIP neuropathologist. It had identified my tumor as "low-grade," or benign, but with "atypical features." The "atypical features" suggested that my tumor could be more aggressive than most.

That alone seemed good reason for another pathology report. Partington said he'd send my files to Sloane-Kettering Cancer Center in New York as soon as possible. He'd also get an evaluation of treatment options.

In the meantime, I felt relieved I had escaped making a decision.

Dear Emmy,

In the last few days you've found it punishing to be with me, hour after hour, as I lie in pain on the couch, so Mommy made arrangements for you to spend the day with friends. When you left this morning, I felt a pang of regret as I watched you drive away, looking out the window of someone else's car, waving goodbye.

In the last few days, I haven't been an especially good father, or husband, or patient. I read and re-read the medical articles I've gathered hoping to find some *answer*, some secret cure that doctors overlooked. Most were discouraging. Even worse, they contradicted each other. One study hailed a new kind of chemotherapy. Another study shot holes in the findings. A lot of articles dealt with small populations of patients—maybe 45 or 50. The patients all had such varied profiles. Some patients had inoperable tumors deep in the brain. Some, like me, had tumors that seemed entirely removed. Some patients had chemotherapy. Some had radiation therapy. Some had both. Some patients were old. Some were my age.

After a while I had trouble making *any* sense of the statistics. Disease, in some ways, is universal. In other ways, it's extraordinarily personal. Disease has a way of becoming entangled with *life*. With plans and aspirations, attitude and will.

The more I looked at these studies the more I wondered about the lives of these patients whose struggles and deaths were recorded on sloping lines.

One study showed that Patient X died nine months after

diagnosis. There it was on the graph. Life. Treatment. Death. Conclusion.

But I began to wonder *how* Patient X died. How much Patient X suffered. Whether Patient X had a family. Whether Patient X regretted the treatments that extended life just a month or two.

Friends drop by a lot to give me what I call Cancer Miracle Books or Medical Miracle Books.

These are books by people who "beat" cancer or AIDS or MS or connective tissue disorder. Some conquered disease by becoming Christian. Others by becoming Buddhist. Some recommended massive amounts of Vitamin C. Others suggested Laetril.

Some books were interesting. But many offended me. In some, there was an undercurrent of *blame*, a suggestion that if you didn't beat the disease you didn't follow the program closely enough or didn't *believe*. Death was punishment.

One of Mommy's oldest friends suggested I get books by Norman Cousins, a writer who had essentially claimed you could stave off disease and death with laughter. For some reason, the Cousins books stuck in my craw. His basic premise—that positive thinking helps your body fight disease—seems reasonable to me. But after making that point, Cousins goes on endlessly, writes volumes on the importance of laughter, without delivering one laugh line.

These books had their own graphs and miracle stories. What galled me was that disease, especially terminal disease, is so individual that "miracle" stories can be found to support any premise. People seemed to beat the odds, whether they were chanting, praying, or laughing. It was the nature of the beast. Some people died suddenly. A handful lived.

A neighbor up the street, Pat, was diagnosed with colon cancer three years ago with a worse prognosis than I have. For a time, it seemed he'd live only months. Pat went through four surgeries, including a colostomy, and went to Washington, D.C., for experimental chemotherapy.

Pat's attitude was bad, by any description. After doctors

discovered his cancer, he grew sour and depressed. He just sat out on his porch eating potato chips and drinking whiskey waiting to die.

But he didn't. After a year or so, he told me that he realized, "Hey, maybe I'm going to be around for a while."

Of course, nobody's going to mention Pat in the cancer miracle books. But there he is, Patient Y, who beat the odds in that first year with chips and whiskey.

This onslaught of books and articles kept me focused on my illness, on treatments and philosophies, on techniques for extending life.

Maybe because of that, Mommy and I really haven't talked much. Not *really*. We've talked about radiation and research. We've both read Medical Miracle books. Yet the research and these books seemed to distract us from our real fears, from our real sorrow, even from our real love and hopes.

This morning, as I sat on the couch, the books and articles that had me transfixed suddenly seemed irrelevant, useless, distracting. What does it matter what statistics say? What comfort can I take in them? Soon I'll become Patient X on somebody's chart. Where on the chart? I don't know.

Mommy came to the couch and sat next to me. She took my hands. We looked into each other's eyes. For several long moments, Mommy didn't speak. I knew we hadn't talked because we were scared to hear what was on the other's mind.

As Mommy sat looking at me, I saw the eyes I remember from so many years ago, in California, Greece, and Mexico, beautiful light brown eyes flecked with yellow. Mommy's eyes glistened.

"I love you *so* much," Mommy told me.

"I love you, too," I said. Tears welled up in her eyes.

I tried to pretend I didn't know what she was thinking. "What's wrong?" I asked.

Mommy tried to keep from breaking down. "I don't want to be left *alone*," Mommy told me. "Please don't leave me alone."

It was like a knife to my heart. Mommy leaned over. I wrapped my arms around her. I ached to tell Mommy she never *would* be alone. But I knew I couldn't promise that. I couldn't promise anything.

"I'm so sorry," I told her. "I'm *so* sorry."

Sunday, June 7

Dear Emmy,

Today you and I had a lazy Sunday.

Emmy, you've been so sweet since I came home from the hospital. You won't do anything to hurt my back. Sometimes you've treated me more like a patient than a daddy.

I know this is haunting you. Last night, you dreamt that the house fell down on top of you. In another nightmare, monsters came and took you to the hospital. For weeks now, you've been waking well before sunrise. Mommy's exhausted, trying to comfort you, trying to take care of me, and having to work at the same time. Mommy's had as many sleepless nights as I have, as many worries, as many nightmares.

Because of my back, I really can't get out of bed and pick you up and give you the comfort you need. Still, I feel a need to do *something* to help Mommy. So last night, as you were getting ready for bed, I told you that if you woke early you should stay in your bed reading books. I asked you not to wake Mommy.

Over and over, I asked what you could do if you woke up early.

"Books!" you blurted out.

I thought you might resist this, but you seemed happy to have me take charge.

This morning, Mommy and I woke with the sunrise. We both felt rested. It was probably the first full night's sleep Mommy's had in weeks. As we sat up in bed, I heard a sound. The sound of paper rustling.

I got out of bed and went to your room to see you sitting up in your bed, flipping through the pages of one of your books. You looked up at me and smiled.

"I'm reading my books, Daddy," you said.

From then on, you appeared more settled than I'd seen you since before I went into the hospital.

Mommy had some chores to do and you and I spent a good part of the day together. In the afternoon, I started to wear down. I made up a snack, a "picnic," you called it. We went upstairs to watch a movie, *The Little Mermaid.*

You and I lay side-by-side on the bed, watching and snacking. Ariel, the Mermaid, fell in love with a human prince. She loved the prince and wanted to marry him. But to do that, she'd have to become human herself. Ariel didn't want to become human because she knew she'd never see her sisters or her father again.

As we watched the movie and cuddled, we talked about the story.

"Someday," I whispered to you, "you're going to have a family of your own."

You looked at me, clearly not understanding. "What do you mean?"

"You're going to have a family and children and a life of your own."

When I said that, your eyes filled with tears.

"But I'll *miss* you, Daddy," you said. "Please stay with me when I get older."

Monday, June 8

Dear Emmy,

Mommy and I had a fight.

I've been trying to walk a couple miles each day to rebuild my strength. Today, as Mommy and I left the house together to walk, I felt trapped and confused.

I don't know exactly what hit me. I started to feel as if I've accomplished nothing in my life. That I had compromised everything. That I was leaving nothing behind.

The feeling's almost impossible to describe. I suppose I've always fantasized that I would leave some mark. That I could point to something at journey's end and say, "That is what I accomplished."

Early in my life, my accomplishments seemed tied to work. When Mommy and I came to Virginia, I had a shot at a job at *The Los Angeles Times*. I turned it down so Mommy and I could have jobs in the same place. Mommy's made similar sacrifices. Over the last six years, as we've stayed in one place, I've watched friends go on to the *Philadelphia Inquirer,* the *New York Times*, and *The Wall Street Journal.*

I'll see the name of a friend on the front page of *The Wall Street Journal* and I *know* that I could have made that choice, too. Still, I never believed that climbing from newspaper to newspaper would make me happier. I remember one reporter in Florida, Faye Joyce, who got a job at the *New York Times*. For a while, she was covering a presidential race. She was often on the front page. But then after the race ended, I stopped seeing her byline. I didn't hear until years later that Faye had committed suicide.

I've always felt comfortable making sacrifices. I made them

for the love your mommy and I share. And now my love for you. I wouldn't trade that love for any job anywhere.

Yet, today I felt I'd wasted my life completely. I'd compromised on my job. I compromised my life.

Mommy didn't get it, in part because I don't think I got it. I don't know if I *get it* even now. I guess I wanted to do something bold. Or *good*. I felt I wanted to do something not because I was drawing a salary for it. I wanted to do something because. . .I don't even know.

I feel tormented. Not just professional torment. But personal torment.

In the last few weeks, everything I believe has been challenged. What struck me, when I woke up in the hospital, and afterward when I came home, was how little I cared for matters that seemed so "important" and "urgent" before my illness.

As we walked, these thoughts and emotions came pouring out of me incoherently. My confusion wasn't all tied to my job, but in a more practical way it was. At my job, I have life insurance. It's not a lot of life insurance—I didn't expect to need it so soon—but it should allow you and Mommy to keep our house. It may also help pay for your college. Clearly, nobody will ever insure me again. So, in a sense, I feel bound to my job by a life insurance policy.

I'm also bound to my job by a disability policy. If I become disabled, my job will pay 60 percent of my salary until I'm 65—or until I die. That's a logical reason to stay put.

But staying at my job means going back to 12-hour days. It means three weeks vacation a year. It means giving up any opportunity to do anything else with the remainder of my existence.

A big problem is, I don't know how long that remainder will last. If I go back to my job and *survive* for another 20 years, tied to a job because I was afraid of dying, I know I'll be bitter. If I quit my job with the idea of doing something else, then get sick again in three months I'll be just as bitter—and broke.

Mommy got defensive. My emotions were garbled. Mommy and I ended up shouting back and forth at each other. I felt angry that I couldn't articulate what I was feeling. But then, I wasn't clear about what I was feeling.

What was evident was that if I went back to my old job I'd be there until I died. Whether in two months or ten years. It sounded so *small*.

Tonight, after you and Mommy fell asleep, I stayed up all night, worrying about everything, feeling caged. I lay next to Mommy in our dark room, watching TV, with the volume low, flipping channels until past one o'clock. The reality just washed over me. My life was ending. Maybe not tomorrow. Maybe not in two years. Maybe not even in ten years. But the end was in sight. To me, life had always seemed a journey. I pictured the journey ending decades down the road. I envisioned living to be an old man. Now, it seems, I'm at the final leg of my journey.

What drove me crazy was that the journey seemed so short. The journey just flashed by. I'd put off so many dreams and promises. I always believed I'd have enough time in my life. Now it seemed it was suddenly too late for my dreams.

As I turned channels, I came across the 700 Club, Pat Robertson's money-grubbing evangelical news program.

Tonight, they had one of their usual "miracle" stories. This story was about a born-again Christian who escaped death when a drunk driver plowed into his bedroom. Of course, this was considered a miracle. He was saved by Jesus because of his faith.

The 700 Club always struck me as crepe paper Christianity. I turned to the monologues of Arsenio Hall and Jay Leno. I watched Nightline for a few minutes, but I couldn't focus.

Then, as I flipped back through the channels, I saw Sheila Walsh, Pat Robertson's Scottish sidekick, making some kind of plea.

Staring at the camera, she said she understood that there were genuine tragedies in life. That people—even Christians—really die. That tears and sorrow are real. That death is *real*.

Christ, she said, offers companionship. He is willing to stand at your side through sorrow. He understands. She opened the Bible to one of the Psalms of David, and in her Scottish accent, read:

> The Lord is my shepherd, I shall not want;
> he leads me beside still waters,
> he restores my soul.
> He leads me in paths of righteousness
> for his name's sake.
> Even though I walk through the valley
> of the shadow of death,
> I fear no evil;
> for thou art with me;
> Thy rod and thy staff
> They comfort me.
> Thou preparest a table before me
> in the presence of my enemies;
> Thou anointest my head with oil,
> my cup overflows.
> Surely goodness and mercy shall follow me
> all the days of my life;
> and I shall dwell in the house of the lord
> forever.

As she finished, the show went back to money-grubbing and prayer lines. I shut off the TV.

I thought about the Psalm. Somehow, in the dead of the night, the notion seemed so beautiful. Not salvation. But companionship. To have someone, anyone, walk with you.

To believe.

To believe that we don't die alone. That love endures. To believe that someday, somewhere, somehow, Emmy, we'll be together again.

Dear Emmy,

Today, my editor, Dave, dropped by to visit for a couple hours. Technically, at the newspaper he's my boss. But we're good friends, too. Dave was one of the only people from the newspaper to be in the hospital waiting room while I was in surgery.

Dave, who has called almost every day, has made it clear he would like me to return to work.

"I'll feel a lot better when you get back in here," he said, "and you probably will too."

Soon after I got out of the hospital, I told him that I wanted to take vacations with Mommy—Christmas, Easter, the summer— so we could spend more time together.

"Well," he said thoughtfully, "you get three weeks."

It was clear he didn't understand—I may live just two years here. Or five. Either way, three weeks a year doesn't add up to much.

Acquaintances don't seem to appreciate the seriousness of my illness. I still get cards from people saying, "I'm glad everything went okay." But, increasingly, it's becoming clear that things didn't go okay. They went better than feared, but this disease is still terminal, is still expected to kill me in the near future.

I guess people are confused because I tend to be upbeat on the phone. Even after surgery, I was able to talk, to joke about my tumor and my scar. People just assumed—well, he *sounds* okay.

Besides, when people ask how you're doing you're supposed to say, "Fine." There seems to be a kind of unwritten pact, a code of silence when it comes to matters of illness and death. People are considerate enough to ask how you are, but fully expect you to lie if the news isn't good.

This creates a kind of schizophrenia. If I tell people the truth, they back off, because they don't want to hear the truth. So I repeatedly find myself telling the convenient lie—that everything was okay. Sometimes it seems as if I'm dysfunctional, worried about a disease that nobody else considers too serious. For Mommy, it's worse. People continually tell her to cheer up, saying she's overreacting. Of course, they have no idea what we're going through. They don't know that she's been unable to sleep. They don't know the real prognosis. They don't understand that, in so many ways, this illness is harder on her than on me. If I die, I'm just gone, but Mommy has to live on, alone, widowed, raising you.

It's gotten to the point that I bristle when most people ask "How is it going?" because I know so few really care or want to know.

When Dave visited this time, I made it clear that we still had a lot of issues to resolve before I was ready to go back to work. I told Dave that I might have to undergo radiation therapy.

"But I thought the tumor was benign," he said, sounding shocked.

"It is." I explained that doctors told us the tumor would probably come back, mostly likely within two years, and that it will probably kill me.

"I always thought 'benign' meant you *lived*," he said sadly.

"Yeah," I said, "so did I."

Sunday, June 14

Dear Emmy,

Tonight Mommy went to see a friend. At bedtime, I read you a story, "Grandfather Twilight." As I left your room, you began to cry.

"Mommy didn't give me a kiss or a hug," you said.

"That's okay, Emmy," I told you. "I'll make sure she gives you a kiss when she gets home."

"No, I want a kiss now," you said.

"Emmy, Mommy's not here," I said.

You continued to sob, inconsolably.

"I'll give you an extra kiss and hug," I told you.

"No," you said. "I want Mommy."

I didn't know what to do. You cried for about fifteen minutes. I was exhausted and my back throbbed. Life doesn't stop when you get sick. Small conflicts just loom larger.

"Ok, Emmy," I said, coming into your room. You looked up at me with those brown eyes spilling tears. "I'll *pretend* to be Mommy."

I could see your look change, just a tad, as you pondered this strange idea.

"I'll pretend to be Mommy," I said, "and I'll give you a kiss and a hug, OK?"

You looked slightly confused, then said, "OK."

I told you I was Mommy. I kissed you on the forehead and gave you a big hug. You calmed down. In a few moments you were asleep.

Dear Emmy,

My neurosurgeon called today.

A month has passed since my surgery. Somehow, the passage of a month makes no sense to me. It seems a day. It seems a year. But one month?

The call somehow stirred everything up again. In the weeks I've been home from the hospital, I've managed to re-establish some of the routine of life.

My back is still painful, but the pain has become less disabling. I now walk a couple miles a day to get back in shape. I also spend a lot of time reading a lot of trashy novels.

Of course, I never *forget*. And Mommy seems obsessed about getting the third pathology report. After a pleasant day of reading and walking, she walks in from work and asks the same question: "Did you get the pathology report?"

My mother, dad, sisters, brother, and friends constantly ask about the report, too.

To me, though, this Sloane-Kettering report serves as a welcome distraction. I can't really do anything until the report arrives.

I suppose there's a part of me that would be comfortable if this report never arrived. With those first seizures, "medical" issues that once seemed so concrete, objective, detached, based in biology and chemistry, collided with my life and eviscerated my hopes and dreams. I found myself sucked into a world of nightmares, irrational fears, haunting doubts.

The absence of this report allows me to hold those medical issues at bay for a while. Of course, the report won't change anything about my medical condition. Whatever is in my brain is in my brain. This report won't change that. But somehow, as long as nobody gives me that final diagnosis, I can act as if everything's on hold, as if even my tumor is waiting for word from New York. Which, of course, it isn't.

Mommy sometimes mentions the possibility of radiation therapy. This report allows me to change the subject. "Well," I'll say, "we'll have to wait."

Partington phoned to say doctors at Sloane-Kettering wanted to examine MRI scans taken of my brain before and after surgery. Partington Federal Expressed the scans to New York. Results probably will arrive by the end of the week, he said.

When Mommy came home, she asked: "Have you heard from Dr. Partington?"

I told her he'd called. I also lied a bit. Although Partington said the results would come in at the end of this week, I told her we'd hear something next week.

During this time, I figured, she might stop pestering me about the report, reminding me of issues I prefer to ignore as long as I can.

Dear Emmy,

God, my back hurts.

I woke up this morning with my lower back so cramped it hurt to breathe. Strangely, my back has aggravated me more than the brain surgery.

I've heard people suffering other illnesses talk about pain, but it's impossible to understand pain if you haven't felt it. Pain can't be touched or measured. Doctors can't see or touch pain any more than I can. When I tell them I'm in agony, I have to put on a pretty convincing show if I want painkillers.

Today, my back is as bad as it has been since surgery. I don't know why. I have to struggle to get out of bed or get out of a chair.

"The brain tumor I can handle," I joked to a friend. "It's the back pain that's going to kill me."

Sometimes I can tell how upset you get when I shout out in pain. Tonight, I decided to sleep on the floor, figuring that hard surface might help my back. In the middle of the night I heard you scream. You were having more nightmares. Mommy brought you into our room to sleep.

So there we slept, side by side on the floor, our heads just a foot or two away from each other. At one point, I opened my eyes to see you staring at me.

Dear Emmy,

I feel as if I've lost my purpose in writing to you. After all, the purpose of these letters was to let you know who I am. But I've always had a hard time writing about my own life. At newspapers and magazines some people write about themselves all the time. They write about playing softball or pickup basketball. They go on elaborate vacations, and return with neatly packaged stories about what they did. I could never picture walking the streets of Paris dictating stories in my head, making choices designed to make a better "story."

In our years together, your mommy and I have traveled over a good part of the world. We've been to England, Wales, Belgium, France, Germany, Luxembourg, Austria, Copenhagen, Italy, Greece, Turkey, Haiti, Martinique, Jamaica, Guadeloupe—and many more places. For me, these trips weren't part of a story I was writing. They were *adventure*. They were *life*.

That's what makes me feel so bad right now. This brain tumor is a big deal. But you have to know—this isn't *me*. This is something that *happened* to me, something threatening to destroy the person I was before. Sometimes I remember that day on the train in Mexico, that old couple, so in love. Will Mommy and I ever be in Mexico again? Will we ever be an old couple at all?

I have a friend who lost the use of his legs and right arm when he was about 35 years old. Today, he gets around in a wheelchair. He once told me the toughest adjustment was growing accustomed to the fact that people never see him as he sees himself. They don't see the life that he lived for so many years, in which he was strong and healthy and athletic. They only see a man in a wheelchair.

He told me that when he dreams he walks and runs. Then, he wakes up in bed with his paralyzed legs, wishing that, for just one moment, he could *be* that man in the dreams, and wishing that somebody else could at least *picture* him running.

Today I wonder—will you be able to see through my illness, through all this trauma, through death even, to see the person who still lives in *my* dreams?

Friday, June 19

Dear Emmy,

Tonight I realized I've become consumed by illness. When I learned that my life would be shortened, I found myself looking at you and feel a pang that I might not be able to see you grow up. So I'd say something to you about my desire to live. At the same time, our house has become cluttered with medicines and medical paraphernalia. The house now seems "sick" to me.

When I mentioned this to Mommy, she agreed. We decided that we really had to get on with *living*. That became even clearer when you were brushing your teeth. You and Mommy were in the bathroom. Mommy was quizzing you on our phone number and our address.

"What number do you dial in an emergency?" Mommy asked.

"Nine-one-one," you answered. Then, after a moment, you added: "That's what you did when Daddy got sick."

"That's right," said Mommy.

Then you looked in the mirror at some redness in one of your eyes. You looked worried. "Am I sick?" you asked.

Monday, June 22

Dear Emmy,

Today, we went to the zoo. This was our first outing together. Of course, I wore my back brace and a hat. Still, I felt like I was a father again, not just some lump lying around on a heating pad, worrying about living or dying.

When we got home, Mommy cooked a fancy meal and we all sat in the dining room. After dinner, I washed the dishes while you went out to play in your new sandbox.

As I did the dishes, Mommy came and asked if I could remove the film from our camera. I've shown Mommy how to remove the film a million times, but she never remembers. She doesn't have to remember. Mommy is always aware that I'll do it. I didn't want to be morbid, but I mentioned to her that she'd have to learn to do this herself, that I might not always be there.

"You don't think I've thought of that?" she said. She walked out and started to cry. Suddenly, it all came back. I thought of all the other chores around the house: We need to paint our house, inside and out; We have to clean the garage; Every fall and summer, I have to seed the lawn. These chores will never really be "done." They will always come up, one after another. With me in the house, I'm able to handle them. But what about Mommy alone?

Later in the evening, I started to feel queasy. My head started to pound and I felt cold and shaky. I swallowed a Nuprin. The more I thought about it, the more it seemed like a regular sinus headache. My eyes were itching too. But it terrified me. What if something were happening?

Before I climbed back into bed, I went into your room. You were fast asleep, a little angel. I want so much to be remembered.

Tuesday, June 23

Dear Emmy,

Today I went with Mommy to pick you up at day camp. When you saw me, you ran toward me shouting, "Daddy!" All three of us went out for ice cream. When we got home, I remembered a kite with a blue unicorn on it that we bought before I was sick. You and I went out to a small park nearby to fly the kite.

The day was warm and windy. Neighborhood kids played soccer and football nearby. A TV crew came by to take shots of ski boats and turned the camera toward us. Your kite went right up and snapped in the breeze hundreds of yards above us. I hunger for days like this. You and I can't really talk yet, but there's a communication between us that has more to do with flying kites than with hospitals or doctors and illness. Your joy seemed so intense, so complete, as you held the string of your kite and watched it cut through the china blue sky.

All my friends and relatives, through, remain obsessed with the Sloane-Kettering pathology report.

"Why is it taking so long?" one of my sisters asked.

"As far as I'm concerned, no news is good news," I told her. "If I had a malignancy I'm sure they wouldn't take this much time. It's probably sitting on someone's desk, waiting to be typed up."

I'm still convinced that it won't show any malignancy, but once the report arrives Mommy and I must make a decision about undergoing radiation therapy.

Nobody seems to understand that I'm not really looking forward to getting this report. As long as it remains in New York,

I'm free from making hard decisions. In this case, I cherish the silence. Silence means I can just go on living.

I'm free to enjoy flying a kite with you, Emmy, imagining that these days with you will stretch out forever.

Dear Emmy,

Today, you, Mommy, and I went to the swimming pool at a community center. I wore a hat, even in the water. My head looks awful. I don't have much hair in the front, where the doctor shaved my head. A scar zigzags across it. Indentations sink in where the surgeon drilled four holes in my skull during surgery. When I'm inside our own house, I don't think about it much, but in public, I wear a ball cap to cover my scar.

Shortly after we got in the water, you pulled my cap off my head, as a joke. I noticed people looking at the scar. "Give me the hat, Emmy," I told you. You thought it was a game. You were laughing, backing up. "This isn't a game, Emmy. Please, give me my hat."

Mommy took the hat from you and gave it back. I acted nonchalant, but there was something humiliating about this.

Suddenly, I recognized one strong reservation about radiation therapy is my fear of being disfigured. Today, my head looks bad, but all this is temporary. My hair will grow back and should cover most of my scar.

Radiation could end forever looking "normal." The radiation would scorch off the hair on the right side of my head, where the beam focuses, my doctor said. The hair, most likely, would never grow back.

The idea frightens me more than I'd like to admit to anyone, even to Mommy. Over the last few days, I've been increasingly aware of the power of beauty. The other day, a woman jogged by, thin and tan, with a long ponytail. She looked so wholesome. She was flawless, young, healthy.

In our culture, it is a common fantasy for persons who are disfigured to be loved by someone young, healthy, and beautiful. Recently, you, Mommy and I went to see the Walt Disney movie *Beauty and the Beast*. In the movie, a prince is transformed into a hideous monster. Eventually, a young, beautiful woman ends up in his castle, held hostage by the "beast."

Later, she falls in love with the beast and kisses him. Her love transforms the beast back into the handsome prince. They are married.

We saw this movie before I became ill. I didn't think too much about it. But, in retrospect, I wonder: Would the story have been as powerful if the woman had been unattractive or old or infirm? Would the story have been as powerful if the prince remained a beast?

Many similar themes run through literature. In Molière, Cyrano DeBergerac loves a beautiful girl. Cyrano is intelligent, but is disfigured by a huge nose. The woman he loves, he is certain, would want to love a handsome man. So Cyrano ends up writing poems for someone who is less intelligent but physically perfect.

Are there any stories or myths about two flawed or disfigured people coming together and falling in love? Could a love story like that create the same power?

Realistically, though, we are surrounded by people who are old, infirm, and disfigured. Back when I was studying at the University of California in Berkeley, I heard people talk about a professor everyone called No Face. No Face, rumor had it, was a chemistry professor. An experiment exploded and acids literally melted his face. He remained on the faculty, everyone said, but he only did research because his face was so revolting. Students claimed he came to the university at odd hours, so he wouldn't be seen.

Late one night, while I was studying for an exam, I went to the library to find a book. I punched the button for the elevator and waited. When the doors opened, I looked straight at a man whose face seemed melted. I felt a sense of shock, or horror, as if I had encountered a monster. I realized almost instantly that this was No Face, the one I'd heard about, but I became speechless, paralyzed.

I suspect he recognized my shock. As he walked from the elevator, he held up a black binder and shielded his face. He walked past me and went outside into the dark.

Of course, I told everyone I had seen No Face. I never saw him again, but I often wondered about him.

Obviously, the man was intelligent. He probably had earned a doctorate. Students all said he was on the faculty of Berkeley, one of the nation's best schools. His face had nothing whatsoever to do with his soul or his intellect. And yet, among students, he was No Face, this anonymous monster.

What had happened to him? I wondered. What did he look like before the accident? Did he choose at first to be so secretive, or did he only later come to recognize the discomfort his appearance caused? Did he have friends, loved ones, parents, children, a wife who could see the man beneath the mask? Did he ever dream of his unscarred face, as my friend in the wheelchair dreamed of days he could run?

When I consider going through radiation, that's what scares me. I won't be the person I am any more, but the man with the hair scorched from his head.

William Butler Yeats once wrote, "bodily decrepitude is wisdom." When I first read that poem I imagined that wisdom came gradually, inevitably. Decrepitude, I imagined, evidenced passage of years. Now, I wonder: Is it possible that decrepitude holds secrets that confer wisdom? Is it possible for someone who is young, healthy, and beautiful to be wise? Intelligent, yes. But wise? And if decrepitude is wisdom, what about disfigurement?

Dear Emmy,

Today I bought tickets for us to go to California to see my family. I've put off buying the tickets because the Sloane-Kettering pathology report hasn't come in yet.

We haven't seen my family in probably two years. This ordeal has been so difficult for everyone. According to my sisters, my mother has taken this hard. I can't imagine losing you, Emmy. It would destroy me. Well, that's what's happening to Grandma. In her mind, I'm still her little boy.

Recently, my sister, Karen, went to a baby shower where people were talking about beautiful babies. Grandma told everyone about the most beautiful baby she could remember. She showed everyone a picture of me.

Friday, June 26

Dear Emmy,

Tonight, Mommy went to see a movie with a friend. I stayed home to put you to sleep and read you a story, the Berenstain Bears' "Messy Room."

I realized how rare it has been recently for me to read to you at night. My back hurts so much that Mommy has read to you most nights for these past weeks. Tonight you cuddled into the crook of my arm as I read.

After you went to sleep, I rubbed my hand along my temple. I felt a small hard nodule, about the size of a BB. What was it? I felt the other side. It was smooth. I didn't want to jump to conclusions, but my heart sank. Maybe this was another tumor?

I've been told that people suffering other illnesses share similar fears. People with AIDS often feel that every cough, every pain, every sore, may be a sign of disease bursting forth. A former editor at the newspaper who suffered a heart attack and who was later diagnosed with lung cancer told me that every time he feels a cramp in his leg he wonders, "Am I having another heart attack?"

I now understand what he feels.

Will such fears ever vanish?

Dear Emmy,

Mommy and I went to see my neurosurgeon today. I assumed Dr. Partington would have the results of the Sloane-Kettering pathology report. When we got to his office, Partington said he had received a list of treatment options from Sloane-Kettering. They included radiation therapy, no further therapy, or chemotherapy.

But Dr. Partington said the pathology report hadn't arrived yet. As we left his office, Mommy acted so disappointed. She has been so tense about the pathology report. Now, we were left in the dark again.

"Listen," I told her, "one of the treatment options they suggest is *no* radiation. That wouldn't be an option if my tumor were malignant. Right?"

"I don't like to make assumptions," she said.

"Well, it seems that wouldn't even be an option if the tumor were malignant. We don't have the report, but it's pretty clear that it's *not* malignant."

"He didn't *say* that."

"Okay, I'll call him and ask him, just that. Okay?"

I didn't.

Dear Emmy,

This morning I woke up feeling melancholy, remembering a place I lived years ago, a kind of refuge. After a semester studying in Paris, France, I found myself broke but didn't want to return to the U.S., so I hitchhiked to an old castle I'd heard about near the Swiss-French border, a castle being renovated by a woman from Paris.

The castle, Pierre Chattel, was built in the ninth century by Charlemagne. A fort above the castle had been converted into a monastery.

Although I'd never met the lady of the castle, nor the monks, they agreed to give me a job, at first cutting wood and milking goats. Later, they asked me to come to the main castle to work on the renovation, under the supervision of a stocky Frenchman with a crude wool coat and a gigantic head with hair that bristled like a brush.

Monsieur Ovine did most of the errands for the lady who owned both Pierre Chattel and the monastery. He drove old Renaults, but his erratic driving had left mangled remains of other cars scattered around the castle grounds.

I fell in love with Pierre Chattel. It overlooked a bend in the Rhone River and lorded over the valley below. It had running water that came from a tremendous underground reservoir, as large as a half-dozen Olympic swimming pools. I moved into a stone cottage with a rough-cut wooden loft. It had a kitchen, if you could call it that, where I kept goat's yogurt, eggs, and vegetables. One window—actually a rectangular hole in the stone wall—looked over a field of wheat.

One summer morning, I looked out the window to see the silhouette of a man harvesting the wheat with a hand-held scythe. I watched him move slowly through the field, sweeping the blade as wheat noiselessly wafted to the ground. By evening, the field was clear, rolled into bales.

The man with the scythe left on a dirt path winding into the hillsides. A few days later, I walked down the same path, where I found an old stone village, with no roads and no cars, whose water spurted from a natural spring in the village center.

Monsieur Ovine and I became friends. On days I had to work, Monsieur Ovine strolled from the castle to my stone cottage to wake me. One night, the lady of the castle gave Monsieur Ovine a horn to summon me. The next morning I jumped awake as that horn blasted out a few feet from my head. I explained to Monsieur Ovine that he was supposed to blow the horn from the castle. He grasped that immediately, but that wasn't the kind of thing that would occur to Monsieur Ovine without an explanation.

It wasn't that Monsieur Ovine was dumb. Far from it. He showed me a library that he had been maintaining in the castle, a library that included huge, hand-written books in Latin and Old French dating back to the days of Charlemagne. Monsieur Ovine also maintained a collection of books and manuscripts about a French mystic and explorer, Charles Eugene de Foucauld.

De Foucauld was one of the first Europeans to find a path across the Sahara Desert. After many other adventures around North Africa, he settled in an oasis in the Sahara, where he was assassinated in 1916.

Monsieur Ovine's dream was to retrace the steps of de Foucauld. Some day, he told me, he would leave the castle to begin his quest. He repeatedly pleaded with me to join as his second in command.

In the meantime, we both worked like slaves. Monsieur Ovine was as strong as a bear. Frequently, when the lady of the castle had men visit from Paris, Monsieur Ovine seemed compelled to show off. As the *Madame* would be entertaining, Monsieur Ovine would walk by, in his heavy wool coat, sweating and grunting, lugging boulders to impress her.

During one of these displays Monsieur Ovine's threw his back out. The injury was bad enough to leave him bedridden. He made his bed in the library, where he lay for weeks, reading ancient books and manuscripts, including the books about his hero, Charles Eugene de Foucauld.

When the summer ended, I left Pierre Chattel to travel Europe and eventually returned to the United States. I often felt a sense of nostalgia about the castle, about the richness of the characters, about the wonders of living in that stone cottage. I've often thought about, and quoted, a line from a book I read while I lived there. "Of the thousand forms of life," wrote Andre Gide, "each of us can know but one."

Somehow, that line stuck with me, resonated. In so many ways it seemed so true, in other ways false. My own life began with so many options. Maybe I could have followed Monsieur Ovine into the Sahara Desert. Maybe I could have remained at the castle. What I did, I did. That can never be changed. The life I choose is the life I live.

Still, those months at Pierre Chattel left me with a comforting sense that I could never become truly trapped. No matter how badly I fouled up my life, I could always escape, always find contentment by returning. Pierre Chattel provided me a kind of fail-safe. I left there determined that I would never do anything in life that made me less content than I felt there. If I don't like the life I live today, I always told myself, I must choose another.

Now, I feel melancholy as I recall those days and realize I probably never will see the castle again. I could return to Pierre Chattel to elude many things, but not illness, not death.

Friday, July 3

Dear Emmy,

Tonight you spent the night with two friends. When Mommy told you this afternoon, you jumped up and down, shouting, "I'm going to spend the night, I'm going to spend the night!"

You ran downstairs and packed your pink backpack with toys and a "special dress," as you called it. When your friends' parents pulled up in front of the house, you ran out the door. Without looking back at us, you walked right to the van, climbed inside, sat down and buckled your seat belt.

"I think she's excited," I said to the other parents. They laughed.

Mommy gave you a quick kiss on the cheek. As you sat there, ready to give me a kiss, I asked, "Are you *sure* you want to go?"

"Yes, silly," you said. As the van pulled away, you turned in your seat to wave at us. I saw your tiny brown hand, waving in the van's back window.

It was a milestone. One of the events parents include in a baby book. Emmy's first night sleeping at someone else's house.

Later that night, Mommy and I lay in bed and watched a movie in which a woman was getting married. The minister asked who would give the bride away.

This was another milestone, another ritual.

Daddies give daughters away.

There are so many milestones in life. The first step. The first word. The first bike ride. The first day of school. The first date. Later, there are graduations, weddings, baby showers.

I remember so well the first time you laughed. Mommy bought you a Mylar balloon and tied it to your crib. Mommy knocked down the balloon. As it floated back up, you laughed out loud. Mommy hit the balloon again and you laughed again. We laughed uncontrollably because you were laughing.

I've always imagined myself entwined in the rituals of your life. That's parenthood. As Mommy and I watched the movie and the minister asked who would "give away" the bride, it tore at me.

Will I live long enough for that ritual? Or will someone have to stand in, explain that your daddy had died?

Dear Emmy,

Today you returned from your sleep-over with dark circles under your eyes. You said you and your friend stayed up all night talking.

"About what?" I asked.

"Nothing," you said.

I asked you again and you shrugged.

I've always wondered what three-year-olds talk about. What did I say when I was three?

I remember my friends and I used to make "plans." We'd talk about making robots. We pictured ourselves at the center of a great drama. We felt that we were keepers of great secrets. Our mothers and fathers knew the neighborhood by street names, but we had different landmarks—the pump yard, the crawl space under Maury Joe Nipp's house, and Ruben's hideout.

Ruben's hideout was nothing more than a drainage area next to a road. To anybody passing by, it appeared a knot of scrub oak and berry vines, but inside it opened up into a tree-covered cathedral. Ruben's hideout was supposed to be a secret. I remember, growing up, wondering about this guy Ruben. Was there a real Ruben? If so, what was he like? I knew nothing about him, but imagined that, if he did exist, he would be a kind childhood brigand, a Tom Sawyer or Huck Finn.

Now, I watch you develop your own secret world, with your own landmarks, like the "secret beach" up the road. To you, our neighborhood is populated by your friends and their anonymous parents. "Look," you'll say. "There's Meredith's mom." Or "There's Emmy Marie's dad." I watch you form connections, this body of myth and fact that will become your life. I long to know more. What are the stories you tell in the dead of the night? I ask, but you won't tell me, any more than I would tell my parents about Ruben's hideout.

Late tonight, I looked in your room to see you sleeping soundly. Probably dreaming. About what?

Dear Emmy,

I went to my newspaper office to have lunch with my work friends today. This was the first time I'd returned since I had my seizure. I dreaded entering the building. It was as if I were visiting a life I'd once lived, but that now seemed behind me.

The last time most people saw me I was healthy. Now, my hair was shorn and I wore a cap.

A reporter saw me as I walked into the newsroom.

"You're back," she said, surprised.

"Yup," I said.

"So how are you feeling?"

"Great," I said. "My back's a bit stiff so I've got to wear this." I opened up my shirt to show my back brace. "But I'm feeling good."

"Well, you look good," she said. "When are you coming back to work?"

"I don't know," I said.

For so many people, that was the true test of health. Going back to the job. You proved your health by returning to your desk, to your assignments. These days, for people my age, work and health are bound together in one package. As long as I couldn't work, what good was I? I was like a baseball player with a broken arm, or a football player with a blown hamstring. "When are you coming back to work?" was the same as asking about my health. That was enough. That's what mattered most.

Editors came over, including some I barely knew. They all asked the same questions. How do you feel? What are you doing these days? When are you going to return to work?

"What's the prognosis?" someone asked. I shrugged. One editor came up and started blabbing about Medical Miracles, about people who had malignant tumors, or transplants, or broken legs, or AIDS. Her stories all had the same type of ending: "And he was back at work in two weeks."

They just didn't get it. They just didn't understand. There was something much more fundamental here than going back to work in two weeks. What happens after that? What if I go back to work in two weeks—then die in three months? What about that?

The managing editor wandered over, hovered around, then asked whether I'd be willing to serve on a newspaper re-design committee forming in the next few days.

I felt rage. I wanted to escape. I collected my friends and walked to a cheap Chinese restaurant up the street. We took up a big table and joked about politics, television, and books. Nobody asked about my tumor or my "prognosis." It felt good to be just another person at the table, not a patient.

At the end of lunch, the waitress passed out fortune cookies. I cracked mine open and pulled out the narrow strip of paper with this fortune: "You will enjoy good health." I laughed out loud.

When I returned home I taped my fortune to my computer screen.

Still, that night, I continued to be haunted by the idea of going back to my old life, my old job, my old desk, my old duties.

At three o'clock in the morning, the house was dark and silent. I was too tired to read, too nervous to sleep. All night long, garbled thoughts and anxieties sprang forth, psychic detritus, everything unconnected, as illogical and horrifying as nightmares. I just wanted to shout out "Stop!" To tell my brain to stop churning—but it wouldn't. My brain tormented me, as if it had become my enemy. Finally, about four in the morning I gave up trying to tame it. I went downstairs to the couch and sat alone. Soon, I heard the slap or your bare feet as you came down the stairs. You looked groggy. You crawled into my lap without saying a word. We fell asleep in each other's arms.

Dear Emmy,

Today Mommy and I celebrated our thirteenth wedding anniversary. It was 16 years ago that Mommy and I met in California. Sixteen years since we traveled through Mexico together.

When Mommy got up, she found us huddled on the couch together.

"I want Daddy to dress me," you told Mommy.

"Okay, but I'll do your hair," Mommy said.

"I want Daddy to do my hair."

"No, Emmy. . ."

"Please, please, please, *please*. . ."

Mommy gave in.

You and I went upstairs. You'd laid out a dress the night before. I put it on, laced up your shoes. I realized I hadn't dressed you in almost two months, since the seizure. I braided your hair and put in a bow decorated with a cluster of deflated balloons.

Mommy was taking you off to swim lessons and day camp.

"Happy anniversary," Mommy said lovingly before she left.

"Happy anniversary," I said. I gave her a long hug.

Mommy then said she wanted me to check on the pathology report before she got home. She's still annoyed that we haven't heard anything from Sloane-Kettering.

"If it were anything bad, I don't think they'd take this long," I told her again. "They're probably just waiting to type it up."

But she insisted. Call Dr. Partington.

It annoyed me a bit. Everyone asked about the pathology report.

When I'd come home from a walk and punch the play button

on my answering machine, I'd hear messages from other people as concerned as Mommy.

"Hi, Greg, this is your sister Kay, calling about the pathology report."

"Hi, Greg, this is Mom, calling to say hi and to check on the pathology report."

"Hi, Greg, this is your friend Kevin. I haven't heard from you so I guess that means good news on the pathology report."

After Mommy took you off to camp, I called Dr. Partington. I told him my wife was nervous. I told him she was getting impatient. I didn't want the whole report. I just needed to confirm that the tumor was in fact benign. I just needed to get that element confirmed. For her.

Partington told me that he'd been trying to get through to the pathologists in New York with no luck. He said they hadn't yet told him the results.

Partington said he was leaving for vacation soon and would be gone for two weeks. He said he'd try to get the report before his vacation. I hung up the phone with a sinking feeling.

What if this tumor's *not* benign? But of course, I told myself, it *is*. I had the sense in my gut. Still, it seemed another week or two might pass before I heard knew.

It brought me down. I was exhausted from the night before. But this was our *anniversary*. I knew how much Mommy loved anniversaries. I wanted this one to be special. We'd go out to dinner. We'd celebrate the 16 years we've had together. We'd forget about illness for just this one night.

I went to shower and looked in the mirror. My beard looked ragged, worn.

I decided to shave my beard. I cut the sideburns off first. I looked at myself with a goatee. It looked ridiculous. Then I cut until I had just a moustache. The moustache looked worse, so I cut it off too. I shaved my face smooth.

When I finished, I looked younger, but pale. The spasms between my shoulders made my back look contorted.

When you got home you both were surprised to see me without a beard.

"You look silly," you told me.

Even Mommy seemed unsure about this new look.

"I'll have to get used to it," she said.

Tonight, during our "date," Mommy and I talked and laughed and kissed. We remembered the wonderful times we have shared. We talked about the night before your adoption and the day we drove home from the adoption agency with you in our front seat, our tiny little friend, our third musketeer.

During our evening out, we stopped at a store where I bought expensive pants and shirts.

"You know what I'm doing?" I asked Mommy.

"What?"

"Investing," I told her. "Investing in the future. Investing in *life*. I can't die *now*. I've got all these nice clothes."

We went to a lingerie store and bought Mommy a green silk robe.

When we got home, though, I was completely worn out. I'd gotten so little sleep that I grew ornery. Mommy mentioned the pathology report again. She told me to call before Partington went on vacation. To insist.

"He's doing all he can," I snapped.

"But I don't want to wait another two weeks."

We argued about it.

By the end of our anniversary night, I felt tired and angry. My head pounded again. As my head throbbed, my moods swung out of control. I felt annoyed with myself. Here's what may be our last anniversary and I felt moody, arguing about a pathology report, about something I had no real control over.

I fell asleep tired, sick, angry, feeling very alone.

Dear Emmy,

You and I woke up before Mommy today and went downstairs to the kitchen, where we ate toast with honey, butter, and jelly.

"Daddy, you look funny," you told me. "Where's your beard?"

"I cut it off, honey."

"Did you throw it away?"

"Yes, I threw it away. It's all gone. Why? Don't you like it like this?"

"No," you said. "Put the beard back on."

I looked at the newspaper. The temperature's supposed to hit 100 degrees.

After you and Mommy left for the day, I walked upstairs feeling nauseous, with my head pounding. I turned on our air conditioner but it didn't cut the heat. I lay down to read an Elmore Leonard novel.

About mid-morning, I got a call from Dr. Partington. He had finally received a preliminary pathology report. In a professional, unemotional manner, he read that the Sloane-Kettering pathologists had diagnosed an astrocytoma "with foci of anaplastic astrocytoma."

Anaplastic.

The word jumped out at me.

Anaplastic meant malignant.

I listened stunned.

Anaplastic.

Malignant.

My brain tumor was malignant.

I remembered all those charts and graphs we'd seen at the

medical library. I remembered the graphs measuring life in weeks.

Anaplastic.

Malignant.

Death.

These thoughts collided in my mind.

At the same time, I did my best to hold a calm, cordial conversation with my doctor.

"Well," I said, struggling for words, "what do we do now?"

Of course, the answer was radiation. But Dr. Partington was leaving for vacation so we wouldn't have time to meet. He suggested that I see the radiation specialist at DePaul Hospital and get started on a program of radiation immediately.

"You know," he told me, "my recommendation always was radiation."

I told him I understood. I took a risk. I gambled. I lost. But even as I said that, I felt intense anger. Not at him but at Sloane-Kettering. Why the hell did it take so long? Here I've had an untreated malignant brain tumor for nearly two months.

I'd assumed that the delay was a good sign. I couldn't imagine that they would have taken so long with a *malignant* brain tumor.

I asked whether it would be a good idea to get another MRI before radiation in case the tumor had grown. He didn't think that was necessary. I insisted. Radiation, I knew, had to be focused on the tumor. My nightmare would be to go through a course of radiation only to find that the tumor was growing just outside the part of the brain bombarded.

After Partington hung up, I felt rage. Over the last two months, I'd accustomed myself to living with a benign tumor. The original seizures were like a trap door opening. I'd finally come to feel some control, some sense that I'd landed. I'd come to a place that I could accept. This new pathology report was like another trap door opening. I was in free fall again.

After half an hour, I tried calling Mommy at work, but she

wasn't in her office. I called my dad. I needed to talk to someone. Anyone. Someone who could help buck me up.

When he answered the phone, he seemed cheerful. My dad had been an alcoholic when I was growing up. Since then, my parents had divorced. My father re-married, quit drinking, and took up religion with the passion he'd had for liquor. I told him that the new pathology report came in and that my tumor was malignant. As we talked, he tried to be upbeat. Over the phone, he prayed that I would live a long and healthy life, that I'd live long enough to watch you graduate from college. I struggled to rein in my feelings of doom.

He urged me to stay confident. But even as he talked, I could sense my father's struggle. Several times, it seemed as if his voice cracked, too.

Still, I didn't have time for depression. I had to get appointments and insurance authorizations before Partington left. Within two hours, I had a week of medical appointments scheduled.

In the middle of this, one of Partington's assistants phoned to tell me my MRI films were missing.

"Do you know where they are?" she asked. "The radiologist is going to need those before he begins treatment."

"They're probably in New York," I told her. "Dr. Partington sent them to Sloane-Kettering for a pathology report."

"Do you know if he did it, or if one of the girls did it?"

"I don't know," I said. "But it went to a doctor at Sloane-Kettering." I gave her the doctor's name.

She told me that Dr. Partington's usual assistant was on vacation. She wouldn't be back for a week so I'd have to wait until she came back from vacation.

"I *know* who has them." I told her I needed the films right away, because I had my appointment with the radiation specialist. The woman said she couldn't do anything until Dr. Partington approved it.

"Well, can you ask Partington?" I said.

"He's on vacation," she said.

"He's already left?"

"He's gone."

Now, I felt the anger I'd been suppressing so long. Okay, maybe I'd blown it. Maybe I should have had radiation right off. But now we have the report. Now we knew we were dealing with cancer. Now it was absolutely clear that I needed radiation and here they wanted me to wait until people came back from vacation.

"Can you beep Dr. Partington?" I asked.

She seemed annoyed. "He'll kill me," she said.

"Well, *do it,*" I said. I didn't shout it or say it angrily. But I said it firmly.

A few minutes later she called back. Sloane-Kettering could mail my films or they could Federal Express them, on Monday, if I agreed to pay for it myself. I agreed that they should be Federal Expressed to my home.

It all struck me as odd. Weeks back, Dr. Partington shipped the films up to Sloane-Kettering by Federal Express because my diagnosis was urgent. Then. . .nothing happened. Now the films sat there.

I felt sick to my stomach. About everything. About the fact that I delayed so long. About all the foot-dragging. Terror was so powerful, so uncontrollable, so overwhelming. It seemed to well up from my core, explode, then collapse over me, dragging me down, swallowing me alive. I longed for dull days, for an hour, for a moment, without tears, nightmares or fear.

Before long, I heard our pickup truck pull into the driveway. I looked out the window. The afternoon was clear but scorching. I could see you and Mommy and a little friend getting out of our truck. You'd been excited all week about bringing a buddy home.

Now, I looked out the window to see you three walking toward the house. Mommy lugged her purse and some books.

God, I wanted so much to avoid telling Mommy. For Mommy, the one last shard of comfort would be snatched away. I went downstairs as you three ran in the door.

"Daddy!" you shouted as you ran in. You hugged my leg.

"Hi Kate," I said to your friend.

"Can I put on my bathing suit?" you asked.

"Okay, but get one for Kate, too." You both ran upstairs. Mommy went to the dining room. She was detached, putting her purse and papers away then looking through that day's mail. You and Kate ran downstairs pulling on bathing suits. I helped you with the straps and you ran outside to play on your swing. Mommy still hadn't paid much more than passing attention to me. God, I wanted to keep the news to myself. Let her have this afternoon. Let her have a few more days. One more weekend. After you and Kate ran outside, Mommy asked whether I had a good day.

I stood there. I didn't know what to say.

"What's wrong?" she asked.

She looked at me. I stood trying to figure some way to break this gently.

"What's wrong?" Mommy asked again. I could see the truth dawning. In those seconds, Mommy seemed to unravel before my eyes.

She *knew*.

"The pathology report?" she asked.

I didn't say anything. Her face contorted. She backed away from me, as if she were scared of *me*. "Oh my *god*," she cried. "Oh my *god*." I walked toward her and she backed away more.

"Don't run away from *me*," I said. Mommy stopped and I wrapped my arms around her. We stood in the living room sobbing while you and Kate played on the swing.

"I don't want them to know," I told Mommy. "I don't want them to see us crying." Mommy agreed. And, while you and Kate played outside, we cried for us, we cried for you.

For a little girl losing her daddy.

Dear Emmy,

Mommy and I had planned to take you to Water Country USA an hour from our home. With the new pathology report, Mommy thought we ought to cancel the plans. Somehow, that seemed wrong to me. We had made plans to do things *we* wanted to do. Besides, I needed to get *out*, to do something. I would go crazy staying in the house.

This morning, I told Mommy I wanted to go to Water Country.

"Are you sure?" Mommy asked.

"Yes, I'm sure," I told Mommy. "Let's enjoy the weekend." We decided to spent the night in a hotel.

On the drive to Williamsburg you snuggled between Mommy and me in the front seat. As you slept, Mommy and I talked about everything, almost incoherently. As we spoke, Mommy would break down and sob silently.

Lou Reed, in a song about dying called "Magic and Loss," sang, "Life is good, but it isn't fair." As we drove toward Water Country, I kept thinking about the line. This isn't "fair." I did nothing to cause this tumor in my brain. I can't even blame doctors, or "modern medicine," or pollution, or tobacco, or high-fat foods. Even if I could find someone to blame, I've come to sense that fairness and blame have nothing to do with mortality. None of us *deserve* to die, but we all will.

I hashed over those words, "Magic and Loss." What is "magic"? Life. Life is magic. Somehow today, for all the sorrow, it seemed even *more* magic. But that didn't lessen my sorrow. The more magic our life, the more painful its loss. All my life, I thought joy and sorrow lay at opposite ends of a continuum, with gradations between. I imagined passing from joy to happiness to contentment, slowly sliding along the continuum toward sorrow. Now I could see joy and sorrow twined together, almost indistinguishable. Sometimes Mommy and I find ourselves sobbing because we are so *happy,* and we fear that happiness will end. But even in our sorrow, the joy remains, coexisting. Tears of profound sorrow and tears of profound joy are often hard to distinguish.

It reminds me of friends we know who avoid falling too deeply in love, fearing pain that love can cause. They're right. The more intense the love, the more intense love's loss. Still, I cannot imagine confining my life to those safe, gray zones where one will never experience the ferocious power of pleasure and sorrow. We all must choose, Emmy, but I can imagine nothing more sorrowful than a sorrowless death, a passing unmourned.

For Mommy and me, love has only grown over our years together. We imagined growing old together, drifting away peacefully. We saw ourselves becoming that loving old couple on the train in Mexico.

I can see now that that was illusory. We never looked beyond the image of this couple riding through the Sonora desert, to the inevitable surprise awaiting them. The inevitable surprise awaiting us all. We never envisioned the day one would meet mortality and the other would ride the train alone.

Now, regardless of how long I live, it's clear: life doesn't come with happy endings. In all lifelong loves, one lover must suffer the agony of watching the other die.

In Williamsburg, we checked into our hotel. Mommy and I cuddled, close and intimate. At daybreak, I opened my eyes. Mommy lay close by, staring at me, her eyes red.

"It didn't go away," she whispered to me, her voice breaking. "It didn't go away."

Dear Emmy,

Today we went to Water Country, part of our decision to "celebrate" every moment. As we walked around, you got a cup and started talking into it, enjoying the echo. You pretended it was a telephone, talking in a robotic voice.

"You-and-Mommy-are-going-to-celebrate," you said in your robot voice. I laughed. "That's-all-you-ever-do, celebrate-celebrate-celebrate." Mommy and I laughed.

I took the cup and said in my mechanical phone voice: "Do-you-know-why-we-celebrate?"

You took the cup. "Because," you said, "you-love-the-world."

At Water Country, you spent most of your time in the kids' section, going down slides, walking under umbrella waterfalls. During every moment, my sense of mortality was absolute. So was my sense of wonder. Everything, everyone, looked so novel, seemed a miracle. Because my back hurt, I lay down. As I did I looked up at the pine trees bristling with needles. All I saw was *life*, living things that would be there for years, decades.

At one point, you coaxed me into an inner tube in the kid's pool. You shoved it under a waterfall, laughing long and hard.

You've always had this great, booming laugh. As I came out of the waterfall, I looked up to see Mommy standing about 20 feet away, holding a video camera. I waved toward her. As I did, it hit me. I pictured you two, alone with each other, years from now, watching this video, watching me wave toward the camera. Mommy would tell you, "*That* was your daddy."

Monday, July 13

Dear Emmy,

This morning, you woke up cranky. As you were leaving for school you came over to hug my leg.

"Are you happy or sad?" I asked.

"A little bit happy," you said, "and a little bit sad."

"Why are you a little bit sad?" I asked.

You looked up at me. "Because you're going to be sick again."

After you left, I spent the day calling my brother and sisters and friends to tell them that my tumor was malignant. I called my boss to let him know I wouldn't be coming back to work any time soon. When Mommy ran into people in the neighborhood or at school and they asked about me, she reluctantly told them about the new pathology report.

This illness has been so hard on you. We've done our best to make our lives seem normal, but that's impossible. I guess it always is. Illness isn't something that happens to a person. Illness radiates through entire families, from my mother, to my brother, to Mommy, to you. There's only so much protection we can offer, but you see my scar, you see my back brace, you've seen me in the hospital. You *know* I'm sick, no matter what we tell you.

When Mommy went to pick you up from school, you acted upset. As she attempted to buckle your seat belt, you threw a ferocious tantrum. Then, as Mommy started to drive off, you said, with a touch of terror and a touch of anger, "*Daddy's* going to the *hospital.*"

It wasn't a question. It was a statement, as if you were delivering the news to Mommy. Mommy was surprised. She didn't want to lie to you. "Yes," she said calmly, "Daddy's going to the hospital."

At that, you started to sob. Mommy couldn't do anything to stop you.

Tuesday, July 14

Dear Emmy,

Mommy has a tiny gold heart-shaped locket that opens. Inside are our pictures, cut from photographs taken soon after we met. You've always loved that locket, loved prying it open to see the pictures. You've often asked if you could have the locket. I told you this was a special locket for Mommy.

"Will you buy me a special locket?" you asked one time.

"I'll get you a gold locket when you turn 13," I told you. You've never forgotten that promise.

Now, I'm not sure I'll be alive to give it to you. So today Mommy drove me to a jewelry store to find a locket for your thirteenth birthday.

"May I help you?" asked the lady behind the counter.

I tried to answer—but I couldn't. I got too choked up and walked away.

"We're looking for a locket," Mommy said.

"Let me know if you find anything you like," the lady said. As I came back to the counter, I saw oval lockets and the lockets with cameos. I wanted to get you one in a heart shape. One stood out, a gold heart-shaped locket with pink- and green-tinged gold filigree. I could picture it on you, years from now.

"Let's get that one," I said to Mommy. Mommy called the sales lady over but I couldn't stand there. I wandered over to look at watches that didn't interest me at all. I could hear the lady and Mommy talking. Mommy called over to me. "How do you want it engraved?"

"What?" I asked.

"How do you want the locket engraved?"

I hadn't even thought of that. I pictured you getting this locket on your thirteenth birthday. Of course you'd want some inscription, some message from your daddy. The idea broke my heart. I paused and thought. The idea seemed so sad.

"Just make it, 'Love forever, Daddy.'"

Dear Emmy,

Mommy and I got wrapped up in medical chores today. Doctors ordered another CAT scan. Our insurance company balked. I spent half the day running back and forth to the hospital, arguing with someone or mediating disputes.

You sensed the tension as Mommy and I ran in and out, fielding phone calls, virtually ignoring you. At one point, you called me saying, "Daddy, I have a surprise."

I ignored you as I talked on the phone, trying to signal for you to be quiet.

"Daddy," you said again, "I have a surprise."

"Just a minute," I said as I covered the receiver.

You waited for a few minutes, then said, "Daddy, I *have* a *surprise*." I still had a lot to do but as I finished that phone call I rushed upstairs with you to see your "surprise."

"Close your eyes, Daddy," you said when I got to the door of your bedroom. I grew impatient as I stood outside your room with my eyes closed. You took my hand and guided me into your bedroom.

"You can open now," you said. I opened my eyes to see that you had cleaned your room. You lined all your stuffed animals along your pillow. You put away all your crayons. You even made your bed, pulling the comforter over the pillows. You'd never cleaned your room before.

"Emmy," I said, genuinely surprised, "It looks *so* beautiful."

I bent down and wrapped my arms around you. I guess that's what you've been needing all along.

Dear Emmy,

Today I got a call from one of Dr. Partington's associates. The doctor introduced himself and in a collegial voice asked if I'd been having headaches.

"No," I answered, struck with a sense that something had gone wrong, that he knew something he wasn't telling me.

"Any slurred speech or weakness in your right side?" he asked.

"No," I answered, wondering what he was getting at. I suspected that the MRI showed that my tumor was growing out of control.

"Good," the doctor said. "I just heard from your radiation specialist, Dr. Sinesi, and he said that the MRI shows a fluid build-up." The doctor went on to explain that I had a blood clot in my brain, a blood clot the size of a thumbnail.

"Well, what's that mean?" I asked.

"I'd like to take a look at the MRI to see if it's clinically significant." As he said that, I noted the term *clinically significant.* What he meant was whether or not this blood clot might kill me before the tumor had the chance.

The radiation specialist would send the films and the doctor would decide "if it's something we want to evacuate."

Evacuate. That term stuck, too. They wanted to decide whether I needed more brain surgery. Everything was spinning so far out of control I seemed almost giddy.

"Did the MRIs show any tumor growth?" I asked.

"I can't answer that," said the doctor.

Until doctors decided about the blood clot, I'd have to delay radiation therapy.

When Mommy came home, I told her about the blood clot. Later in the afternoon, Dr. Partington's associate called back to say had received the MRIs. There was definitely a "collection of fluid," he said. He wanted a CAT scan to determine the density of the clot.

"Sometimes the MRI is so sensitive it just lights everything up," he said. As long as I had him on the phone, I asked whether he noticed any sign of tumor growth.

He said there was a sliver along the edge of the surgical area that "lit up" on the MRI, but said I'd have to talk to "Dr. P" when he returned from vacation.

By the end of the day, Mommy and I were near emotional collapse.

Dear Emmy,

Today I went to DePaul Hospital Cancer Center to be "marked up" for radiation. Since my hair had grown in some, I came without a hat, figuring it might be my last opportunity. As I walked into the hospital, I passed other people sitting outside other offices, many looking frightened. As I walked passed them, I felt an empathy I'd never really known before. I saw a woman sitting by one door. Her daughter—who looked sick—slumped across her lap. The lady looked as if she'd been crying for weeks. I wanted to say something to her. But what?

How many other people were there throughout the hospital waiting for some treatment, some miracle? It struck me as strange how little we know about what actually happens in these hospitals. Anyone can rattle on about radiation therapy, dialysis, chemotherapy, surgery, but our knowledge is so schematic, based on snippets from TV shows or news accounts.

Yet hospitals like DePaul are repositories of enormous caches of medical devices, tucked away in hundreds of rooms, floor after floor, each designed for very specific illnesses. Throughout this hospital, hundreds of other patients were discovering other devices, other drugs, making certain that their AIDS treatments or CAT scans or chemotherapy drugs were the best.

When I walked into the radiation waiting room, I looked around at the other patients. One wore a kind of ascot around his neck and spoke by holding a small instrument to his throat. The heavyset lady was there again, wearing sunglasses. I could see mascara streaks on her cheeks. A handful of people wandered in and out. Some seemed cheerful, almost jaunty. But I knew they all had cancer somewhere in their bodies, in their bowels, their lungs, their testicles, their bones, their skin. Somewhere lurked mutated cells that had transformed their lives as radically as mine had been transformed.

After just a few moments in the waiting room, a nurse led me back to an area for "mark up," preparation for radiation therapy. I didn't know what to expect.

The nurse told me to lie on a hard flat table that moved every direction with a hand-held remote control device. When she got the table to the correct height, she shut out the lights. At that point I noticed a ruby-colored glint on the tip of my nose. A series of lasers shone from different directions, creating a crosshatch on my skull.

The nurse got out a bottle of liquid that looked like red ink and painted over the laser lines. I lay, smelling the ink, feeling the cold brush strokes, wondering what I would look like. She then taped a cathedar line to my head. This would make the lines show up on x-ray film, she said.

"Ok," she said. "Lie perfectly still." She left the room to take a series of x-rays. I was in there probably half an hour.

When I walked out, with the painted lines still on my head, I looked toward the receptionist.

"How do I look?" I asked.

"Your daughter's going to think you have war paint on," she said.

The mark-up went faster than I expected. I had asked Mommy to pick me up, but she wouldn't be there for more than an hour. I figured I could walk home.

As I walked from the hospital, though, I could see people look at me. These red crosses lined my head, making me look as if I were the member of some strange cult. I was, the cult of those undergoing radiation treatment.

I walked half a mile to a sporting-goods store, where I picked out a cap. I could sense everyone in the store staring at me, averting their eyes when I turned toward them.

Tonight, as I put you to bed, I showed you the red lines. You thought they were neat. You rubbed the stubble on top of my head.

"Your hair's coming back," you said.

"I know," I told you. "But soon I'm going to be totally bald." I tried to say it as cheerfully as possible.

"Your whole head is going to be *bald*?"

"Yes," I said. "And every night, you can rub it."

"I don't want your whole *head* to be bald. You're going to look *funny*."

"No, I'm going to look good, because I have a pretty head and you're going to be able to rub it as much as you want."

"It's going to look funny," you said. "People are going to *laugh*."

Dear Emmy,

This weekend has been among my lowest.

Before I began radiation therapy I read as much about it as I could. It wasn't encouraging. One Scotsman described radiation as a "my wee sledge hammer."

According to my doctors, my brain will be blasted with radiation strong enough to kill the cancer—along with swathes of healthy brain cells in the vicinity.

"If they weren't doing this to you on purpose," a friend joked, "you could sue the hell out of them."

As I write today, I wonder whether I'll be able to write tomorrow, or next week, or next month, as my brain begins to show the effects of the radiation. My doctor said in most cases, radiation wouldn't do all that much harm. But they'll be blasting the part of my brain that controls language and abstract thought, the part of my brain that is my livelihood.

That does scare me. Writing, even relatively trashy writing, requires subtlety. For a several years, I worked in Florida in an area with intense competition among newspapers, TV stations, and even radio stations. I always listened to radio and TV news programs to follow competitors. In the morning, I read competing newspapers, line by line, to compare our stories.

I was often stunned at how the right word, the right quote, the right angle, adds spark to a story, transforming a routine event into a tale that would end up on the front page.

I loved writing and worked at it. I learned shorthand to capture courtroom dialogue. I studied other newspapers' techniques of attribution. I also benefited from phrases that just kind of bubbled up, without being forced. Those were usually the best. As doctors discussed the "subtle" differences in cognition and speech that most people don't even notice, I wondered whether those phrases and ideas will emerge as easily, whether I'll even be able to continue to write these letters to you.

Dear Emmy,

Doctors called it good news.

They decided to allow me to begin radiation treatments. The blood clot is still in my brain, but the risk of delaying radiation therapy, they figured, outweighs the risk that the blood clot might continue to grow.

As I say, the "good" news comes with a lot of qualifications. But I must admit that I've become anxious to become some sort of treatment.

Today's radiation session—my first—wasn't too different from the mark-up session. Two technicians, Kim and Lisa, escorted me into a room with a linear accelerator, a monstrous device that looks like an oversized x-ray machine. I lay on a hard table, which they adjusted with a remote control so that fixed laser beams would shine along the crosshatch of India ink painted on my head. Once the table was adjusted, Kim rotated the linear accelerator to point at a target point near my left temple. She joked about "zapping" my brain.

Kim and Lisa both left through a huge, heavy metallic door that closed behind them, making me feel as if I were in a vault. I stared up at the beige ceiling tiles, listened to soft pop music, then heard the static hum of the linear accelerator generating power behind my head. Seconds later, the device pointing at my temple made a buzzing noise. I lay perfectly still, afraid of what might be happening to my brain.

In what seemed seconds, the buzzing stopped. Kim and Lisa came in and rotated the linear accelerator to shoot the radiation through my right temple. In just a few minutes, I was allowed to leave.

As I walked back out through the waiting room, I saw two men, one an impeccably-dressed man with bushy black hair, carrying a briefcase. He looked Turkish, about my age, maybe younger. He stood next to an older man, apparently his father, whom I figured he'd brought in for treatment. The son filled out medical forms, stoic, self-assured, as if conducting a business transaction. I could see him looking around at the "patients" almost dismissively. I saw him look at me and knew he was wondering why I was there.

Dear Emmy,

This morning, as I walked out of the radiation treatment room, I saw the Turkish-looking guy across the hall. He was still with his father, still carrying his briefcase. The radiation specialist was showing him an x-ray, pointing to a circled spot. Cancer. Somewhere.

As I passed, he looked my way. He hadn't shaved. He had lost his composure. I knew the moment I saw his eyes—*he* was the patient. For a moment, our eyes locked. The truth had dawned on him. This was *real*.

Feeling slightly nauseous and depressed, I walked outside the radiation area into the main hallway of the hospital. Why was this happening?

Lately, I've felt a lot of anger. Mostly, I've agonized over the fact that I waited so long to begin radiation therapy. Much of my anger was directed at Sloane-Kettering. Why had they taken so long?

In the books and articles my friends gave me, anger is often lauded, encouraged. Patients direct anger at doctors and hospitals and medical personnel. Theirs is an anger born of the sense that, with the right medical care, the right doctors, the right nurses, the right medical gadgets, we can escape suffering, can escape this defining characteristic of the human condition, our mortality.

It's easy to blame doctors. They are trained in the science of fixing the body. As such, they sometimes view the body as a machine. They order MRIs without knowing what it's like to be in the throat of that monster. They sometimes discuss "side effects" as if patients dream them up.

The truth is, my doctor, my hospital, all those nurses and technicians—whatever their shortcomings, real or imagined—saved my life. Without them, I wouldn't be alive.

No, my anger digs deeper. It is born of fear. Fear of dying. Fear of suffering. Fear of separation. Fear of abandoning loved ones. Fear of being forgotten. Fear of having squandered this, my only life.

I'm not sure why this confrontation with mortality has shaken me so badly. I've always known death lay in store for all of us. When I lived in South America, that seemed especially obvious. Widows often mourned for years, wearing nothing but black even to neighborhood *fiestas*. Funeral processions wound through our residential neighborhood, a custom forcing acquaintances to recognize someone's passing. There was a small *tienda* near out apartment that sold candy, ice cream, and coffins. Death was undeniable, woven into the fabric of life.

When I got back to the states, I noticed how death seemed sequestered, disguised, tucked away. Cemeteries here look like parks. Funeral homes seem stately mansions. Public mourning is frowned upon.

Still, in my own life I've never had the luxury of ignoring death. As a police reporter, I often arrived at crime scenes along with police to see bodies—shot, stabbed, or, in one case, crushed by a bulldozer. Later, when I covered medicine, I spent several weeks in a children's ward and watched as premature infants died despite herculean efforts by doctors and nurses. When children died, nurses shielded the incubator and the family behind a cotton screen covered with colorful cartoon figures.

Of course, cartoon figures could never lessen the agony of parents whose children lay dying. Death can't be gussied up.

Mortality makes all other "important" matters seem paltry. Once, years back, I watched a well-to-do tax attorney stand at a courtroom podium wearing a costly, well-tailored silk suit. As he delivered a closing statement to a U.S. Magistrate, he stopped mid-sentence, as if he had a catch in his throat. I looked up to watch him fall backwards, in slow motion, onto the carpet, where he lay, staring up at the ceiling, seemingly unconscious, gurgling. Deputies rushed to revive him, but I could see the color drain from his face. Time stopped. I noticed the handful of other people in the courtroom, the stenographer, the prosecutors, the client, staring, stunned. What had happened? This morbid intrusion into an otherwise routine hearing seemed so imposing.

Paramedics arrived. I watched as one used scissors to cut off the lawyer's tie, then cut open his silk coat. In the futile effort to save him, they ripped open the lawyer's white, broadcloth shirt. The attorney probably would have been furious if someone had spilled coffee on his suit that very morning. Now, the game had changed. His suit, no matter how expensive, was no longer consequential.

Mortality, thrust upon us, forces us to question everything we value, expensive suits, good jobs, nice cars, power, prestige, fame—writing. I remember one of my uncles who swore he didn't want to live if he were so ill that he couldn't snow ski. Yet, when he came down with liver cancer, he clung to life for all he was worth.

For me, that's been part of the trauma. In my life, what endures? What matters? What still seems important? My job at the newspaper isn't even in the top ten. It frightens me that I may come out of treatment unable to write or think. I sometimes wonder whether my surgery has already caused damage when they scooped out some of my brain during surgery. But today, that issue doesn't seem as monumental as I might have expected.

All that seems to matter, to really matter at a gut level, is compassion, brotherhood, friendship, parenthood, love, these nebulous emotions we forget so often, but which grow so important toward journey's end.

As I walked out of the hospital, I walked past two rooms I have seen every morning. But somehow, on this morning, they fascinated me.

In one room, radiologists gathered to examine x-rays. Doctors kept room lights low to allow them to examine x-ray films clipped over a wall of fluorescent light. I looked in at shadowy figures, silhouetted by fuzzy black-and-white negatives of brains, necks, lungs.

Just beyond that room, I passed the chapel. A priest knelt before the alter. Soft light streamed in through red-and-yellow stained-glass windows.

This morning, I was struck by the likeness of these two rooms, these two chapels.

Dear Emmy,

Today you and Mommy and I went to see the movie *Honey I Blew Up the Kids*. Through the movie you sat in my lap, holding the bag of popcorn, fixated on the screen.

After the movie we came out into a thundershower. We rushed out and climbed into the pickup truck, soaked. Mommy pulled out into the traffic and I could see cars backed up as sheets of rain came down. The rain reverberated on the truck, as if pounding on a tin roof.

"Let's play a game," I said, shouting over noise of the storm. "I'll tell you my favorite part of the movie, then you tell me your favorite part of the movie, then Mommy tells us her favorite part of the movie, and then we start over."

You still didn't seem to be paying attention.

"She's not going to be able to do that," Mommy said.

"Yes she will."

I told Mommy that, but I wasn't really convinced.

"My favorite part," I said, "was when the baby got so big and he was walking through the street and he picked up the car because he thought it was a toy."

As I spoke, you paused, listened, and nodded.

"My favorite part," you shouted over the sound of the rain, "was when he was in the kitchen and he went near the microwave and a blue light came on and he got bigger."

"I remember that," I said. "That was funny."

Mommy told one of her favorite scenes. Then it was my turn again.

"My favorite part was when he got so big and his shoeslaces

were untied and a truck drove onto his shoelace and he fell and he saw all these tiny people around him, like they were toys."

You nodded. "*My* favorite part," you said, "was when he was in the other room and everyone saw him and he was big and they screamed and ran into the other room."

Mommy said a favorite part. "Okay," she said, "the game's over."

"No it's not," I said.

"My favorite part," I continued, "was when the baby tore off his door and his daddy said 'Give me the door' and they were fighting and the baby bonked him on the head." You laughed.

"*My* favorite part," you said, "was when he was in the car and they were trying to hide him from the mommy."

"That was good," I said. You nodded.

Mommy laughed. Here we were, riding in the truck through a thunderstorm, having what amounted to a conversation. Since the seizure, we've focused so much on my medical condition that we've missed that fact that you're still growing up, getting more mature. Months have passed, and in those months you've learned to talk so much more clearly, to hold conversations.

"Emmy," Mommy said, surprised, "you remember so much."

Thursday, July 23

Dear Emmy,

I went to lunch with some friends at the newspaper today. Jim, a former editor who has had lung cancer, arrived at about eleven in the morning.

"How are you doing?" he asked as I climbed into his car. "I hadn't talked to you since the dire news."

It surprised me. I seemed I'd talked to him just a few days ago. But as I thought about it, everything had happened so quickly. I'd gotten the "dire news" just a few days back. I told him I was doing okay, starting radiation.

"Well, you sound like you're taking it well," Jim commented.

I shrugged. "Yeah, I guess so."

Jim told me that when he first was diagnosed, his wife remarked how well he had taken the news: "I told her, 'What's the choice? I can do this, or I can put a gun to my head.'"

We headed downtown; I stopped to give some blood and to arrange for more referrals for my appointments in a month.

As we walked through the newspaper building, everyone seemed busy, rushed, wrapped up in "important business."

One editor I barely knew walked over. "So, how are you doing?" he asked.

I told him things were hectic, that I had spent the past week rushing from one doctor to another without any break. "Today," I said, "is my most relaxed day in a week."

"No doctors' appointments," he said.

"Well, only two," I said.

I left the building feeling that I didn't fit in any more. All these editors and reporters were running around working on "important stories" or "important committees."

I know most of the editors and reporters. Many work late into the night. Some have children, children they see only on weekends or for a short spell each night. Many acknowledge that they're making sacrifices, but believe those sacrifices are justified, offset by the "importance" of their work. Besides, hard work might lead to something better. A better salary. A better job.

I looked at them and saw myself three months before. There were times I'd work straight through lunch and dinner, well into the night, then jump at the chance to cover a late-breaking story.

I remember I used to hear a siren, or see an ambulance, and wonder whether there was some story I should chase. Now, I hear a siren and I feel a pang of empathy, of fear really, fear that someone might be suffering. "Let them be okay," I think. The "story" is the furthest thing from my mind.

Today, I had a hard time seeing how issues these editors and reporters considered so "important" could ever be important to me again.

Dear Emmy,

Today Mommy took me for my daily radiation treatment. As I walked in, I heard the nurse at the front desk congratulating a woman who was "graduating," meaning she'd finished her treatments. I got a kick out of that. When I've thought of illness, of cancer, or radiation, I've never thought of "graduating" from treatment.

The notion seemed encouraging. To graduate. To have another credential, such an important credential, marking a crucial juncture in one of life's most intense, most frightening passages.

Someday I would "graduate" too.

"When I graduate," I joked to Mommy, "I want to have a graduation party."

"It's a deal," she said.

Saturday, July 25

Dear Emmy,

This afternoon, you, Mommy, and I headed for King's Dominion, an amusement park about three hours from here.

I've never been a big fan of amusement parks. Still, Mommy has wanted to get out of the house, get away, find something that would make you happy that wouldn't tax me too much. We decided to drive up, spend a night in the hotel, then go to King's Dominion.

When we got to the hotel, all three of us snuggled up watching TV. After you fell asleep, Mommy lay next to me.

Mommy had been somewhat moody all day. "I'm so scared," she whispered to me. "I can't live without you. I want you to be with me forever." She started to cry.

I cradled her. I guess this was the first time I've felt capable of offering comfort to Mommy.

"Everything's going to be okay," I said, trying to convince her, trying to convince myself. "Everything's going to be okay."

Dear Emmy,

As we walked from our hotel toward King's Dominion this morning, you pointed to one of the rides.

"Look," you shouted. "*Toys.*"

At King's Dominion, you went wild, going on every ride. You never grew tired. I was grateful to be alive, watching you sitting at the wheel of a jalopy, or coming down a water slide. Mommy and I had only one motive, to see that you had a good time.

In so many ways, Emmy, I've grown to know you so much better because of this illness. When I worked at the newspaper, I attempted to have "quality time" with you. Now it seemed that the "quality time" was just a lame attempt to jam parenthood into short, intense blocks. Since I've been recuperating we've spent hours and hours of *unhurried* time together. We've become friends. Could I have gotten to know you this well if I'd remained healthy? I don't think so.

At one point, you ran over to a game where people win stuffed animals by shooting a water gun at a target. I've never done well at games like that.

"Daddy, could you win me a surprise?" you asked. "*Please?*"

"No," I told you. "That costs extra money."

"Please, please, please, Daddy."

"No, honey," I said. "If I play, it doesn't mean I'll win."

So we stood and watched other people playing. I told you we could go back to the rides, but you wanted to stand there watching. Whenever somebody won, you turned to me again.

"Daddy, win me a surprise," you said.

Suddenly, you burst into tears. A woman behind the counter leaned over and whispered something to you.

"I want my daddy to win me a surprise," you told her, sobbing. This wasn't the phony cry you sometimes make when you want something. You somehow seemed agonized, hurt. Even the lady at the counter seemed touched. I leaned over.

"Emmy," I said. "Even if I play, I probably won't win."

The lady reached under the counter and pulled out a small stuffed alligator. "Here you go," she said.

You took the alligator and thanked her. As we walked away, you handed the alligator to Mommy.

"Don't you like the alligator?" Mommy asked.

You shrugged. It was clear to me. It wasn't that you wanted a stuffed animal. You wanted me to *win* you something. Anything. "Give me two dollars," I said to Mommy.

"If you don't win," Mommy said, "you're going to break her heart."

"I know," I said. I sat down at a horse race game, in which you advanced the horse by shooting a water gun at a target. I had horse number 14 and competed against a dozen people.

As the game started, I heard you cheer.

I pointed at the target and shot without watching the horse. I heard a lot of commotion then a bell.

"*Number* 14," the carny said.

"Daddy won!" you shouted. "Daddy won!" I couldn't believe it. I'd never won anything like that. You picked out a colorful stuffed clown. "Clowny," you called him.

You were so proud. You carried Clowny with you the rest of the day. You walked up to another girl, showed her Clowny and said, "My daddy *won* this for me."

For you, today, your daddy was magic.

Dear Emmy,

When Mommy and I woke up in our hotel room this morning, we looked over to see you sleeping in white tights and ballet shoes, with your arms flung over Clowny. Ah, you are so beautiful.

During the weekend, the three of us connected as we hadn't in months. When you woke up, I looked toward you and Mommy. "Hey, I've got an idea," I said.

"What's that?" Mommy said.

"On Emmy's tenth birthday, let's come back to King's Dominion."

Mommy gave me an odd look.

"Emmy can bring two friends," I went on. "We'll get adjoining rooms. Never mind the expense. We'll have a room to ourselves and the girls can have their own room. And their own TV."

"But Daddy," you said. "We won't be able to *reach* the TV."

"But you'll be bigger then."

"Oh," you said with a sense of wonder. "And we can knock on your door?"

"It's a deal. You can knock on our door."

Mommy didn't say anything.

"We've got to do it," I said. "Emmy's tenth birthday. It's definite."

Mommy still didn't say anything.

"That's only seven years," I told her. "We can make it seven years, right?"

Mommy smiled and squeezed my hand.

"Definitely," she said.

Tuesday, July 28

Dear Emmy,

I've learned the pattern that will govern my life for the next month. Every morning, at 9:15, Mommy takes me to the hospital for radiation, which lasts just ten minutes or so.

The schedule has modifications. On Monday, doctors check my blood, to make sure the radiation isn't depressing my immune system. On Tuesday, radiation therapists tape diodes to my hair to check the strength of the radiation. On Friday, I meet with one of the radiation specialists.

That may not *sound* routine. To me, it makes sense. I know where I'll be throughout the week. No more rushing around making appointments. My life, at least for this month, has fallen into a comprehensible pattern. It's something I can understand, something I can depend upon.

Once radiation stops, though, the pattern changes again. From what I can tell, I won't be seeing doctors for months at a time. I'll be at home, alone, trying to pick up the pieces of my life, returning for an appointment every three months.

This, I guess, is pretty standard for people suffering serious illnesses. You are returned to life, as if on a medical furlough.

I wonder how I'm going to handle everything then. In the past couple months most of my concerns have been *medical.* Now, I'm starting to get a sense of a different battle ahead. Whatever happens, whether I live or I die, my life has changed. I find myself not only wanting to *live,* but to live differently. I want to take back those parts of my life that I've surrendered.

A lot of that comes down to work. Today, when I think of the newspaper, I think of money. I make a good salary at the newspaper, more than Mommy makes as a college professor. I have excellent benefits. Once the salary, insurance, and other benefits seemed secondary to the fact that I enjoyed my work. Today the salary, the disability insurance, the life insurance, seem like anchors.

Do those benefits make it worth going back to a job that no longer stimulates me? To a life that no longer interests me? And for how long? A year? Two years? Ten years?

I have always thought that one day I would make a break. Now I wonder: If this isn't that day, will there ever be one?

Dear Emmy,

Last night I called my friend Peter, in Seattle. Peter and I had known each other since high school. We met when he and his older sister Ann were joking about their alcoholic father. Everyone laughed. After they told one story and started laughing, I said, "That's not funny." According to Peter, they *knew,* instantly, that my father was a drunk, too. They knew that I recognized the pain at the core of their stories.

From that moment, Peter, Ann, and I became friends. When my parents got divorced, I didn't really mention it. When Peter's dad died, he didn't say a word. Still, there was a strange bond between us.

At the end of one summer, Peter and Ann went to Florence, Italy, to spend a year studying. They sent me postcards, describing German beer halls and the art in Italy. I decided to go to Europe to study, just like them. I arranged to study for a semester at the American College in Paris.

I didn't know anything about Europe or about any part of the world, other than California and Mexico. In college and high school, I had concentrated on math and music. I arranged to fly to Frankfurt, Germany, because the flight was cheap, but I had no idea what to expect.

My sister Gail, in an effort to be helpful, invited me to her house and introduced me to someone who had served in the military in Germany. He told me Germany was icy cold, with snow drifts and frigid winds. He told me to prepare for Siberian conditions. I went to a camping store and bought wool pants so thick you might wear them to climb the Himalayas. I also bought clunky, calf-high rubber boots with wool inserts to insulate to 20 degrees below zero. My plans were simple. I'd fly to Frankfurt, Germany, and hitchhike to Florence, Italy. I'd then hitchhike back before classes started in Paris.

I remember, vividly, the day I left for Europe. I sat at the departure gate at the airport, surrounded by businessmen wearing suits, carrying briefcases. They looked toward me wearing my wool pants and boots, looking hot. I thought to myself, "They have *no* idea what they're in for."

Of course, I sweated miserably on the plane trip to Germany. When I arrived in Frankfurt. . .well, I was shocked. The sun shone, it was near 70 degrees. I lugged a backpack full of clothes intended for blizzards. I had almost nothing for a sunny day and no shoes other than these sweltering rubber monsters.

Over the next few days, I got my first lessons in living abroad. I found myself in restaurants looking at menus that I didn't understand at all. I'd point to the menu, or sound out a word, and hope they'd bring me some sort of sausage. Once I scanned the menu looking for something I could afford. I pointed and the waiter shook his head. "*Nein,*" he said, German for "no." I figured he wanted me to get something more expensive. I continued pointing at the menu. He continued to shake his head in an emphatic no. I insisted. A few minutes later, he brought me what I had ordered—a large plate of mustard.

I hitchhiked south, toward Italy. In southern Germany, I got a ride with a Rumanian. He didn't speak any English but in hand signs, nods, and a kind of charade he managed to communicate that he'd drive me all the way to Italy if I told customs officials that I owned something in his trunk. I didn't understand, so he opened his Fiat's trunk to show me a large slaughtered hog. He seemed to feel it was unlikely that we'd be stopped, but he emphasized the point that I had to pretend that *I owned the hog.* I didn't see any harm in that.

We headed south. During the trip he sucked down cigarettes, lighting a new one with the butt of the last one. Once, he offered me a cigarette. I had never smoked. I waved my hand, indicating that I didn't want the cigarette. He insisted. I said no. He continued to insist. He became offended. It was impossible to communicate that I didn't smoke. Finally, I took the cigarette. He lit it for me and I found myself puffing away, driving through the Swiss Alps. Occasionally, he'd look my way, hold out the cigarette and nod, as if to say, "Pretty good, eh?" I nodded. In northern Italy, he stopped for gas. He ran into the store and returned with an entire carton of Marlboro. He forced me to take them.

I arrived in Florence, slightly nauseous from smoking, lugging a heavy, overstuffed backpack, still wearing my wool pants and my blizzard boots. When I arrived at Peter's apartment, I must have looked like a character from a bad cartoon. We laughed for hours. He suggested I abandon my boots but I was reluctant because I didn't have anything else to wear. We walked through Florence, eating pizza and spaghetti, drinking capucinno, wine, and beer, sampling the delicacies of Italy. We walked across the Ponte Vecchio, the "old bridge." I saw Michelangelo's David, and the other statues he'd carved during the same period, statues of men attempting to struggle free from blocks of stone.

Too soon, I left Florence for Paris. In Paris, I bought some cheap French hightop sneakers and rented a room in a seventh-floor garret. I loved everything about Paris. I loved the Notre Dame, Eiffel Tower, the stalls of book sellers lining the Seine. I loved the cheap bottles of red wine in plastic bottles, the French bread, the pastries, and the paté.

At 19 years old, new vistas opened. The world I discovered was far more varied, far more wonderful, than I had ever imagined.

Over the years, Peter and I had sent each other hundreds of letters. After Mommy and I joined Peace Corps, Peter joined too, and went to Africa for three years.

At one point, though, there was a rupture in our friendhip. Peter's older brother, Stevo, was hit by a car and died. I remember when I heard that. I had no notion how Peter felt. I wanted to write or to call but I didn't have any idea what to say. I actually scribbled out a few letters, then threw them away. For a couple years, I didn't call, I didn't write, I didn't communicate with him at all out of fear of saying the wrong thing.

Death and illness have a way of doing that to people.

When I had my supposedly benign brain tumor, people sensed that my medical ordeal would be *contained,* come to a resolution. Once I got the report of malignancy, friends Mommy and I have known for years quit calling, quit visiting.

When I recall how I reacted to Stevo's death, I understand that silence isn't necessarily malicious. Death and illness have a way of paralyzing the healthy. Because they don't know what to say, they say nothing.

Today, I phoned Peter to tell him that the tumor in my brain was malignant, that I didn't know how long I would survive. I wondered how he would handle it. Any better than I had so many years ago?

Thursday, July 30

Dear Emmy,

Today I got a call at home from one of Mommy's colleagues. When I answered the phone, he seemed stunned, almost speechless. He cut the conversation short, saying that he really wanted to talk to Mommy. "Hang in there," he said. Then he phoned Mommy at work.

"Is there anything we can do?" he asked Mommy, a question we've both heard a thousand times.

"Yes, there is," Mommy said. "You can invite us over."

He never did.

Saturday, August 1

Dear Emmy,

Tonight a thunderstorm rolled in. I listened to the rain pound on our slate roof. The thunder and lightning kept me up for a while then I drifted off.

I was back at work, at my old job, my old office, my old desk. My editors asked me to go to a municipal building to look up records. When I got to city hall it was full of nurses and doctors and lab technicians. A nurse rushed over and said she needed to see me right away. She took me to an x-ray machine, focused it on my neck and said my cancer had spread to my throat.

"I thought this kind of cancer didn't spread," I said.

The nurse shrugged. She pointed to an x-ray.

"Right there," she said, pointing to a transparency. I couldn't see anything.

"They'll have to cut out your throat," she said, calmly.

I ran out of the building, got on my bicycle, and rode away panicked. I awoke with my heart pounding in my ears, then I heard the rain. It was only a nightmare, I told myself. I lay in bed, in the darkness, listening to the rain, afraid to go back to sleep.

Dear Emmy,

This evening, you and Mommy and I went to the College of William & Mary to have a picnic. I've always loved William & Mary's campus with its brick buildings, walls, and courtyards traversed by brick walkways.

While Mommy set up the picnic, you and I roamed. Near the edge of a campus, underneath a tree, you came across a white bow, the kind you attach to birthday or Christmas presents. The bow sat under a tree, next to a plaque that read "In memory of Hazel Sloane, 1893-1986." The plaque jarred me.

You grabbed the bow. I pointed out the plaque and told you to leave the bow there, that it was probably left in memory of the lady, Hazel Sloane.

"Did she get dead?" you asked.

"Yes, and this plaque was put there by the people who loved her. So they can come and see it."

"Was she a mommy?" you asked.

"I'm sure she was."

You looked at the plaque and at the tree. "Is she that tree now?"

"Well, yes. Her spirit's in that tree."

"If we cut down the tree, will she be alive again?"

"No. We can't do that. She's dead. She can't come back to life any more."

"She's going to be dead forever?"

"Yes," I said. "She's going to be dead forever."

We started talking about the bow. I was sure someone just dropped it. But I wanted you to understand that people often leave things in memory of loved ones.

"Did they leave this for Sloane?" you asked.

"Maybe they did."

"But if we don't take it, somebody else will take it," you said. You looked up at me, pleading.

"No," I said. "Good people will leave it there."

"Only bad people will take it?"

"Yes," I said.

"But Sloane won't know," you said. "She's dead."

"Well," I said, pointing at the plaque, "how would you feel if this were for Daddy? And you brought flowers for your daddy— and someone came and took them?"

You paused for a moment.

"I'd go to their house and snatch them back," you said in an angry tone. "I'd glue them on so nobody would take them." You decided to leave the bow.

We wandered back toward Mommy. It was a cool, peaceful August evening. You looked up at me with your dark brown eyes.

"Are you going to get dead, Daddy?" you asked.

I felt a pang of sorrow and guilt. I squatted down. You sat on my leg.

"Yes, I am, honey," I told you. "Everybody dies someday."

"Is Mommy going to get dead?" you asked. The question caught me off guard.

"Yes, she is, hon. Someday."

You looked at me, not sad, but angry. Stunned.

"And then I'm going to be all alone," you said.

Dear Emmy,

It's begun. For weeks now, I've been psyching myself up for the hair loss that accompanies radiation therapy.

I've had all these notions about how I'd react. Early on I told Mommy, "If I start to lose my hair I'm just going to shave my head."

During last Friday's appointment, my radiation specialist tugged at a couple strands. "You've got strong follicles," he said. The hair was hanging on but he warned me that my hair *would* fall out.

After my morning radiation treatment, I sat reading a book when I noticed three or four hairs drop onto the page. I brushed the hair aside. Then a few more fell.

I reached up to my scalp and tugged on my hair, as the doctor had a few days back. My hair came out. It was almost like pulling weeds. There no resistance, no feeling.

This nauseated me. I'd been preparing for this. I wasn't going to let it get me down. I lightly tugged at a wad of hair on top of my head and it came out as if it had never been attached.

I tried to go back to reading, but I couldn't stop thinking about my hair. I ran my fingers through my hair and more fell out.

I thought about all my efforts to *will* myself back to health, to visualize good things. Try as I might, I couldn't *will* the hair to stay on my head. The follicles were dead.

When Mommy got home, she cut what was left of my hair as short as it's been in decades, about half an inch all over.

As much as I'd prepared myself for this inevitability, I found myself worrying obsessively. Tonight I couldn't sleep. I can't say I had nightmares, because I never slept. I was sucked into strange, endless dialogues. I pictured people forcing me back to work. I pictured waking up and finding clumps of my hair on my pillow. I worried that I'd never see my brother and sisters again. I worried about things beyond my control, that I knew could never happen, but I couldn't stop myself.

I tossed and turned and walked around the house worried.

I drifted off at maybe five o'clock. Soon after, I heard you. You walked over and stood next to our bed. I knew Mommy wanted to avoid having you sleep in our bed. I knew I should send you back to your room. But I was so tired. I opened up the blankets and you crawled in. I drifted off, feeling comfortable, sleeping a silent, dreamless sleep.

Dear Emmy,

Today when I lay on the radiation table a technician taped a diode to one side of my head to measure the radiation dosage. As I lay as still as I could, I thought about the diode. In the past, she taped it to my hair. In the past, when Kim or Lisa yanked it off it hurt.

Now, I knew, it wouldn't. Kim and Lisa left the room and turned on the linear accelerator. I heard its static hum. After a few moments, they returned.

"This is going to hurt a bit," Kim said as she leaned over to pull the diode from my hair.

I didn't feel it. I could see the tacky side of the tape as she removed it. I saw clusters of hair. She saw it, too, but didn't say anything. On the other side of my head, she taped the diode to my skin.

I came home in a funk. I had prepared myself intellectually but it still disgusted me.

In the evening, after you went to sleep, I went with a friend to Cogan's, a nightclub nearby. Friends gathered around the table drinking beer and joking. I sat drinking Coke, wearing my baseball cap. Occasionally, I would catch my reflection in the mirror across the room. I was the only guy in the room with a hat. I knew within a week or two, my hair loss wouldn't be easy to cover.

Soon after I arrived, someone else showed up with two women, both young and attractive. People made introductions.

At one point, I noticed one of the women staring at me. Not just glancing but *staring*. I looked her way, saw her large, brown eyes looking right at me. She didn't even flinch. For a few, slow seconds our eyes connected. A few moments later, she started staring again.

Of course, my hair didn't look strange or patchy. It just looked short. But I found myself wondering if someone had told her that I was sick, that I was receiving radiation treatments, that I had a illness that's most often terminal? What did she know? Was this a stare of pity? Or something else?

The thought haunted me. I imagined a kind of unspoken emotional reservoir in the room. Were people thinking, "He has cancer," and just forcing themselves to be cordial? Were they putting on fronts? I didn't know, but then I'd look across the table and see her staring again.

Dear Emmy,

My hair has continued to fall out in clumps. At first the hair thinned out on top and on the sides, as if I were going bald naturally. By this morning, though, it had come out clean to the scalp on one side. It no longer looked natural. I spent a lot of time looking in the mirror at my strangely elongated skull.

I had lunch with my newspaper friends. I mentioned that my hair was falling out.

"How long until it grows back?" asked one writer.

"It's not going to," I said. "It's permanent. Or at least, it's probably going to be permanent."

"Oh, I didn't know that," he said. I could see everyone register surprise. Losing your hair temporarily is one thing. Losing it permanently is another.

"George Pass's hair came back," said Bob Geske, a reporter I'd known for years. Geske was never one for small talk. I remember that he was close friends with an older reporter, George Pass, who died of cancer a few years back.

"Did he have radiation to the head?" I asked.

"Yeah, his was in the brain."

I thought back to Geske's stories about the death of George Pass. George had lots of good friends. As George's cancer got worse, Geske came to work depressed. George had grown incoherent. George couldn't recognize friends. A group of newspaper people and Virginia politicians threw a party for George. That day, George seemed to enjoy himself. He remembered old stories and old friends.

Soon after, though, George started to waste away. Geske told us George would be going any day now. He was barely hanging on. By the time George Pass died, death seemed a mercy.

I'd always known George Pass had cancer. But there were so many types of cancer. Other types of cancer can spread to the brain.

"Did he have another type of cancer that spread to the brain?" I asked Geske.

"No," Geske said. "It was in the brain."

I grew silent. I thought of asking more. How long was he sick? How did he find out about it? All the questions that I'd learned were important. Before, when I was first diagnosed, knowledge seemed power. Now, knowledge frightened me. Knowledge seemed a curse.

I changed the subject.

At bedtime, Mommy read you a story. When she came into our room, I lay in bed wearing my hat.

"Get that hat off," she said. "You don't have to wear hats inside the house."

I pulled it off. I knew my head looked awful now with the bald patches and my raised, reddened scar.

"Maybe we should just go shave your head right now," Mommy said. "Come on."

"No," I said. "Maybe tomorrow."

"Why not now?"

"I just don't feel like it now. Maybe tomorrow. It doesn't really show with the hat on, does it?"

I put the hat on. Mommy looked.

"No," she said. "It doesn't really show."

"Yeah," I said. "I figure I'll cut it when it starts to show."

I took the hat off.

"I look like a freak, don't I?" I asked Mommy.

"Nooooo," she said. "You're so beautiful. I wish you could see yourself the way I see you."

Just then, I noticed that Mommy had gotten her hair cut. I

complimented her hair. We looked at each other and I started to feel lousy. Mommy could see what I felt.

"Let's just go cut your hair off," she said.

"No. Not today."

Mommy looked at me lovingly.

"It's the shits, isn't it?" she said.

Dear Emmy,

I wrote early in my letters that I didn't want my illness to dominate my letters to you. Since I've started radiation therapy, however, that's been hard to do.

I never expected to have such a traumatic reaction to hair loss. A first, it seemed such a minor complication. Hair loss? What's the big deal about hair loss when we're dealing with life and death? I could handle that.

But I guess I've always liked my hair. A columnist at the newspaper told me about a year ago that he was thinking of buying Rogaine, a cream that's supposed to return peach fuzz to balding heads. As he grew bald he started to get a sense of hair as human plumage.

Once you're diagnosed with a serious illness, concerns about plumage seem vain and superficial. When radiation therapists talk about hair loss you're expected to say, "No problem. I can handle that."

Still, the fact that I am sick doesn't make it any easier. When my boss recently told me permanent hair loss was no big concern, I wondered how he'd feel if he had random swathes cut out of his hair, down to the scalp. I wondered how he'd feel if he woke up with his head shaved entirely.

How many treatments were like this in hospitals, making you sick in the hopes of making you well? Treatments that left people without hair, without vocal chords, without legs, without lungs, without colons, covered with the scars of this battle to forestay the inevitability of death?

How far would people be willing to go to *live*?

At least with my hat on, I looked pretty normal. I looked *healthy*. But once I had my head shaved, I'd look sick. I thought about those kids you see on TV, the kids with the disease that makes them age early. They're usually totally bald, wearing baseball caps, sometimes tipped to the side to look sporty. But they don't look sporty. They look *sick*.

With my hat on, I could *talk* about losing my hair but nobody could *see* it. There was no visible evidence of this illness that had transformed my life.

When I took off my hat and looked in the mirror I was startled. With my hat off, I looked sick. Someone asked me today, "Is your hair falling out normally, or does it look kind of like you're from the Outer Limits?"

"Definitely the Outer Limits," I joked.

After I hung up, I asked Mommy about that. "Yeah," she said. "It's kind of like the Outer Limits."

That stung.

"But you're still beautiful," Mommy said.

It was impossible for me to conceive.

This afternoon, as I walked to Bazemore's Market to buy some food, I ran into a neighbor, Mary, who was pulling out of her driveway. I hadn't seen Mary since she returned recently from a month-long driving trip across the country.

She stopped. Her son Nathan, on the passenger side, rolled down his window. "How's everything going?" Mary asked, leaning over her son to the open window.

Of course, since they'd left for their vacation everything had gone insane. I didn't feel like going into it.

"It's going fine," I said. "I'm hanging in there."

"Are you all through with the treatments?"

"Well, I'm going through radiation now."

I could see Mary register surprise. Last time we talked, I told her I wouldn't have radiation. "Really," she said. "I didn't know. Is that like chemotherapy?"

"No, its like a super x-ray. A beam. They shoot it into your head. I'm about halfway through. I've been going for three weeks. I have three weeks more to go."

"And that's supposed to cure it?"

It was getting to hard to avoid. "No, but it's supposed to kill malignant cells."

"Oh, I didn't know," she said. "I thought. . ."

I tried to be casual. This was a conversation I'd held so many times these weeks.

"Yeah, the other pathology report came in and, you know. . ." I just trailed off.

Mary seemed at a loss for words. It touched me that she seemed so concerned. She said something about Pat, the guy up the street who had had colon cancer, but she didn't finish her sentence. "And so the radiation will kill it, so it doesn't come back?" she asked.

"Well, it won't come back as fast. At least, that's the idea."

Nathan, her son, was squirming. He wanted to get wherever they were headed. He didn't like this conversation. I stood there leaning toward the passenger window, holding my bag of groceries, wearing my red cap. With the cap on, I looked normal.

"Well," Mary said, "at least you're keeping your hair."

"Yeah, down here," I said. I pointed up to the top of my hat. "Up above it's falling out."

I was tempted to pull my cap off but I couldn't. I knew it would shock her. It might even make her mad.

"Well, when they're done your hair will grow back, won't it?" Mary asked.

"No," I said. "It's permanent. Or at least they think it will be permanent."

She registered another shock. I could see it. Nathan by then had lost his patience.

"*Mom*," he said.

"I've got to get going," Mary said. "We'll have to get together sometime."

"Sure," I said.

Mary pulled away and I continued walking under the shade trees of our street. It was a beautiful evening. There were other neighbors out, too. It seemed to me that only you, Mommy, and I knew about this secret under my hat.

Dear Emmy,

Today Mommy and I went to Stark & Legum, a store downtown, to buy a hat for me. I've never worn hats before. I always thought they looked strange on me. But now I *had* to wear them. It wasn't only to cover the baldness. But to cover my scar. I've grown tired of baseball caps but have no idea what kind of hat to wear.

What struck me was how much buying a hat meant making a decision about *image*. Last week, Mommy convinced me to buy a straw panama hat with a multi-colored band. I felt ridiculous, wearing this jaunty, Caribbean hat, when I felt sick. The same day, I bought a $45 Dobbs bleached straw hat with a stiff, wide brim. It looked country-western, but a bit formal.

I've worn the Caribbean-style hat a couple times, when Mommy insisted. I wore the Dobbs straw hat a couple times but it seemed formal and so *big*.

I wanted something else. Something less conspicuous, but not a ball cap.

At Stark & Legum, an elderly store clerk showed us all kinds of hats. Wool snap brimmed hats. Big Stetsons. Hats with feathers poking from the brim. Derbies. Floppy cotton tourist hats.

Trying on hats was like making a decision about my identity. Did I want to be a cowboy? A rakish adventurer? A snooty academic? A sloppy tourist? Did I want to be bold or understated?

I tried on probably two dozen hats. Mommy brought me one that looked like a floppy, upside-down sailor's cap.

"No way," I said.

Over in one corner was a stack of beige canvas London Fog

hats that cost $27. I tried one on and Mommy thought it looked fine.

"We've got other hats with the same cut," the clerk told me, seeming anxious to direct me away from the London Fog.

It wasn't that the London Fog was a *bad* hat, he said. But he wanted to show me *better* hats. Dobbs and Stetsons. The clerk went back into the storeroom and returned with a dark blue felt hat, a Dobbs, with the same cut as the London Fog.

"Now, *that's* a good hat," he told me proudly. He said it ran about $80.

I had discovered another world. I wondered about this world of hats, about people judging others, shrugging, "Oh, *look* at that cheap London Fog."

Still, I bought the London Fog.

When we got home, I looked in the mirror. From the front. From both sides. Mommy said the hat looked good.

But then I noticed that the hat didn't cover all my bald patches. On the left side, a bald patch descended about an inch below the hat line.

"Can you see that bald spot?" I asked Mommy.

"No," she said. "I see a light spot. But it just looks like your hair's gray there."

In the afternoon, I went to a movie with Pat, the guy up the street, to see a new Clint Eastwood movie, *Unforgiven.*

When Pat drove to our house I walked out wearing my canvas London Fog. Pat didn't say a word about the hat. We talked about radiation therapy but I was thinking about my hat. I wondered if it looked odd.

When we settled into our theater seats, I felt self-conscious. The London Fog suddenly seemed too large. I guess it stretched out a bit. It slid down around my ears. I felt as though everyone in the theater was looking at me.

The lights went down and *Unforgiven* started. From the first frames, I found myself distracted by the hats on the screen— broad-brimmed Stetsons, derbies, floppy cowpoke hats.

In one scene, Clint Eastwood and a partner rode horses across the horizon and you saw silhouettes. Eastwood was wearing a broad-brimmed hat. The brim was straight, parallel to the ground. His partner, Morgan Freeman, had a hat that drooped. In silhouettes, the hats seemed perfect for their characters.

Throughout the movie, I watched dozens of hats. Most looked like they were cut from felt or wool. These were *expensive* hats, I thought to myself. They weren't just taken off the rack.

Richard Harris, playing an English dandy and assassin, wore a impeccable black felt hat. Gene Hackman, a small-town sheriff, wore a high-crowned brown hat.

I thought about the $27 canvas London Fog sitting on my head. Truth is, it takes a talent to wear a hat.

When I got back home, I looked at my hat in the mirror. Then I switched back to one of my ball caps that rode low and covered all my bald patches.

Saturday, August 8

Dear Emmy,

Mommy shaved my head out on the patio today. She patiently cut off all my hair then shaved my head smooth. It took about an hour.

While Mommy did this, she cried. Shaving my head was intended to be an act of defiance. I remember talking to a friend drafted to go to Vietnam in the 1960s. At the time, he was playing in a rock band and had hair down to the middle of his back. The day before he reported for induction, he went to a barber. He paid two dollars and told the barber to cut off all his hair.

"I knew I was going to have to cut it," he said, "but I didn't want to give the Army the pleasure of doing it."

That was my logic. Radiation was killing my hair follicles. I was going to beat radiation to the punch.

I went upstairs and looked in the mirror. You don't really know the shape of your head until you shave it. My head was shaped okay. But not great. My scalp, which has never seen the sun, is as white as powder where my hair had been.

Worse yet, shaving my hair made my jagged surgery scar more pronounced. I could see where every stitch had been. In shaving my head, I wanted to do something bold. The truth is, there were no *good* choices. I was choosing the best of bad choices.

Standing at the mirror, I tried on my hats and ball caps. The ball caps looked pretty good from the front. But in the back, there was an open spot above the adjusting strap. I'd never really paid attention to that spot in a ball cap before. Usually hair stuck out of it. Now, just above the adjusting strap, I saw baldness. It unnerved me to see that patch of baldness.

Mid-morning, you and Mommy and I went to a reptile museum. It was my first public outing since Mommy shaved my head. Shaving my head did accomplish something. I was bald. Utterly bald. The sense of hiding something under my hat was gone. Anyone who looked at me could see I had no hair. I didn't have the fear I'd had before about my cap getting pushed crooked, revealing a swathe where the radiation had done its damage.

Monday, August 10

Dear Emmy,

We went rock hunting this afternoon.

Mommy wasn't around and I didn't have any other plans. You picked up a blue gift bag with rope handles. Then you found a Burger King paper cup.

"We can use this to scoop the rocks and then put them in the bag," you said. When you said "bag" you stretched out the vowel as if you were talking about an extremely precious object.

We walked out of the house and you said you wanted to go to the house of your friend Meredith. "She has rocks where the car drives out," you said.

"You're right," I answered, "she does."

We got to the driveway and you bent down with the Burger King cup.

"Hold the bag," you said.

I held the bag open and you dumped in half a cup of rocks. You started to scoop another cup.

"You can only take two cups in each driveway, so you don't leave bare spots," I told you. You didn't even answer. You just stood up and got ready to go find another driveway.

It was hot out. I was wearing my London Fog hat to block the sun, but I could feel the sting of radiation burns.

In the hours that followed, you came up with all kinds of games. Hide and Seek. Duck, Duck, Goose. Colored Egg. Before this illness, when I was working full-time at the newspaper, I wouldn't have had time for these games. This afternoon, there was a magic about being with you. I couldn't sit down on a couch with you and explain illness or loss. You were still my baby girl, too young to have to deal with such issues. But you did understand that Daddy helped you fly a kite and collect rocks. Beneath ran a communication that doesn't exist in the realm of words, but in the realm of feelings, steeped in this bond between a father and daughter.

Later in the afternoon, while you were on the swing, Mike, a reporter for the newspaper, drove by. He stopped as you were taking another shot at climbing a signpost on the street corner. I felt the chemistry of afternoon change.

As Mike talked about the newspaper, about journalism, I felt so distant from that world.

Mike started talking to me about my "illness," like a reporter gathering facts. I'd been a reporter long enough to recognize the forced sincerity and all the mannerisms that were my own months before.

As we sat on lawn chairs in the front yard talking, you walked over and climbed into my lap. You leaned into my chest and listened as we talked.

"I bet you're flooded by calls and visitors," he said.

"No," I said. "A lot of people have pulled away."

You leaned back and cupped your hand against your mouth as if you wanted to tell a secret. I leaned over. You put your hand over my ear.

"Show him your bald head," you said.

I smiled. I pulled back and looked at you. You had a mischievous glint in your eyes.

"Not right now, honey," I told you.

"Show him your bald head," you whispered moments later. I chuckled. For the last couple of days, I've done my best to get you accustomed to seeing me with a shaved, scarred head. For you, it didn't seem to matter. I'm your daddy. You've seemed to have little trouble adjusting to these physical changes.

Now, as you pleaded with me, it was as if showing Mike my bald head would prove what I'd been telling you, that this slick head is neat, interesting.

You reached up to the brim of my hat, not as if you were going to take it off but in a kind of nonverbal way of asking again. I knew what was under the hat—three large, red India ink crosses and a ragged, ear-to-ear scar. It wasn't a pleasant sight. Still, it didn't matter to me what Mike thought. What mattered at that moment was what you thought.

Mike heard these whispers. He didn't know what we were whispering about. But as we talked, I lifted the London Fog off my head. He seemed stunned.

"So is that your. . .Are those your. . ."

"That's where they shoot the radiation," I said, pointing to a red X.

"And that's your. . .That's your scar. . ."

"Yup." I just sat there, in a lawn chair, with my hat off, listening to Mike grope for words as you snuggled against my side.

Dear Emmy,

My brother Doug flew in from California a couple nights ago. Throughout this ordeal, I've been in regular contact with my family. I've talked to Doug, my mom, and my sisters on the phone dozens of times. My sisters ask about my treatment and I keep them posted. I told them when I started to lose my hair but I haven't seen any of them since Grandma left after surgery.

I looked forward to seeing Doug. Doug had visited Mommy and me almost everywhere we'd ever lived. When Doug arrived, Mommy and I stood in the corridor of the Norfolk airport, and I wondered how he would react to seeing me. Finally, we saw him at the other end of a hallway, coming toward us, wearing Levis and new white sneakers.

Doug is one year younger than I am, but he looked so young, so healthy, his hair so *thick*. Seeing him made me feel old and incredibly sick. He saw us and waved.

When he strode up to us, Doug seemed surprised that I appeared relatively healthy. I guess he was expecting to find me strapped to a hospital bed. I remember talking to him on the phone just before he flew out, and he said: "If you have any surprises, tell me now. I mean, if there's something you're not telling me I want to know about it before I get to the airport." I don't know he thought I might be hiding. Maybe expected to find me drooling or in a wheelchair.

Doug did seem a bit put off by my shaved head. He hated when I took off my hat. He didn't like the scar. He had no desire to look at the blistered, dying scalp. But with my hat on, I looked okay.

Since Doug arrived, we've had a couple lazy days.

That didn't bother you. You took a shine to him. As he lay on the floor, you snuggled up against him.

On his second night here, we all went out to a restaurant. You ate with perfect manners, trying to impress your favorite Uncle Doug.

Saturday, August 15

Dear Emmy,

Since Doug arrived, we've been busy. Doug wanted to go to North Carolina so yesterday, after my treatment, we all packed up and drove down. I've been feeling pretty bad. The radiation seems to be taking its toll, sapping my energy, If it weren't for Doug, I don't know that I take this trip.

After we arrived on North Carolina's Outer Banks, we checked into a hotel. Doug wanted to go to to the Lost Colony, which played in an outdoor theater. He wanted to go even though it was drizzling. We went to the play and sat there until a thunder shower drove the entire audience away.

This morning, Doug said he wanted to go hang gliding on the sand dunes of Kitty Hawk, North Carolina. I couldn't hang glide because of my back. The weather didn't look so great. I didn't feel too hot. Still, we headed to Kitty Hawk.

Truth is, I was working hard to do whatever Doug wanted to do, as if attempting to prove I was healthy.

In Kitty Hawk, you and Mommy went to find a hotel room for the night. The afternoon storm cleared up just as Doug and I started to walk up the dunes at Jockey's Ridge for his hang gliding flights. A few drops of rain fell, but on this humid summer afternoon the light rain seemed refreshing.

From the dune's ridge, the view was spectacular. Layers of white, willowy clouds and thunderheads floated along the horizon. Down below, in a sandy valley, a dozen people swam in a fresh-water pond formed by the storms.

Soon after we reached the top of the dune, I heard you screaming for me and looked down to see you running toward us.

You'd never seen anything like this before—a giant sandbox with people hanging from kites.

For two hours, as the sun set slowly behind the layers of clouds, we watched Doug hang glide.

Doug would glide down the hill, sometimes only a few feet above the sand, then walk back up the dune boasting.

Even though I couldn't hang glide myself, I enjoyed watching Doug enjoy himself. It made me feel alive. At dusk, I took you to the lake, where you peeled off your clothes and, wearing only underwear, paddled around the pond.

After we checked into the hotel, the four of us swam around in the hotel pool. You and Mommy were exhausted—I was, too—but Doug wanted to go to a comedy club.

At the comedy club, we were led to the stage by a waitress with a deep tan and a halter top that looked like a push-up bra. Around us were other tourists, including a lot of young women. Doug, who's single, looked around at all the women with their deep summer tans.

"I think I'm in love," Doug said, looking over to one table.

The waitress came over and I ordered a Coke. A Coke cost as much as a beer or a mixed drink, but I can't drink alcohol because of medications I'm taking. If it hadn't been for that, I might have ordered beer or wine.

Doug didn't have any restrictions.

"What kind of whiskey do you have?" he asked the waitress. She shrugged. "Do you have any Black Label?" he asked.

"No, we don't."

"Do you have Johnny Walker Red?"

"No," she said.

"What about Jack Daniels? You've got Jack Daniels, don't you?"

"Yeah, we have Jack Daniels," she said.

"Give me a Jack Daniels and a Budweiser," Doug said.

I have never drunk much hard liquor. Actually, one of my most powerful memories of hard liquor was watching my father chug whiskey years ago. I guess I was about 19. I can't remember what prompted this drinking jag but my dad was incoherent, bawling, talking about how miserable it was to be an alcoholic. He poured whiskey into a short, fat tumbler. Then he guzzled the entire tumbler of whiskey and poured more.

There was nothing I could do about it. He drank until he passed out on his bed. I left him there. I didn't see him for several months after that.

Over the years, friends have given me and Mommy liquor for birthday or Christmas gifts. Those bottles have been under our counter for years now.

It's not that I didn't drink at all. When I lived in Paris, I used to drink wine almost every day. I remember buying wine with a friend, studying price, size, and percentage of alcohol, calculating to make sure we got the most alcohol for our money. Still, I never drank hard liquor.

I've seen Doug drink whiskey, but not that often. As the comedian launched into his routine, Doug laughed along and downed his Jack Daniels, chugged his beer, then ordered another round. I hadn't even finished my Coke when the waitress brought me another one. I remember feeling pressured to finish my Coke. Doug kept the rounds coming.

When the waitress came over after several rounds, Doug asked, "Can I have a cigarette?"

The waitress leaned over me. She was young, probably about 18, probably working a summer job. She smelled of suntan lotion. She seemed confused by Doug's request.

"Can I have a cigarette?" Doug repeated when it was clear she didn't understand. Doug held his fingers up, making the motion of someone smoking.

"I don't have a cigarette," she said.

"Can you get me a pack?" Doug asked.

"We don't sell them," she said. "There's a vending machine in the. . ."

"Can you go to the vending machine and get me a pack?" Doug said full volume.

The comedian, sitting on a stool just a few feet away, looked over wondering what the hell was going on at his feet.

"I don't have any money," the waitress said.

"I'll give you the money," Doug said. He took out a five-dollar bill and put it on her tray. "Camel filters," he said.

She left. She seemed as if she'd reckoned up the options and decided it was easier to buy the cigarettes than argue the point. She came back about ten minutes later.

"They don't have Camel filters," she said.

"Marlboro," Doug said. "Anything."

She left again and returned with a pack of cigarettes and three dollars change.

"You want another Coke?" Doug asked me.

"No," I said. I still had half a Coke left.

Doug hesitated, then said to the waitress, "Give us another round." She walked off.

Doug placed his whiskey on the stage, just a few feet from the comedian.

The comedian, who had been joking about Californians, began to talk about the recession. "Yup, I lost my job." He paused. "Working in a toll booth." People snickered a bit. "Best job I ever had," the comedian said. "Two thousands cars a day, 25 cents a car, I was taking home $500 a day."

Doug burst out laughing then said in a booming voice, "I liked that one." Doug shouted it loud enough for half the club to hear.

The comedian thanked Doug for the compliment.

"I like that one because I work for the state," Doug said out loud.

"Oh, good, good," the comedian said. He then said to Doug, almost off-handed, "Where are you from?"

Doug clearly did not want to become the butt of the comedian's California jokes.

"Lockford," Doug answered.

"Where's that? Pennsylvania?"

"Near Lodi," Doug said.

"Oh, Lodi," the comedian said, nodding his head, as if saying, "Of course." After a pause he said, "Okay, where's Lodi?"

"You know the song?" Doug answered. Then Doug started to sing an old Credence Clearwater Revival song, "Oh Lord, stuck in Lodi again."

The comedian paused and seemed stunned. "Great, great. I asked a simple question. Where's Lodi and he starts singing, 'Lodi, Lodi, good old Lodi.'"

People laughed.

"I can tell you work for the state," the comedian went on. "They come up to you and say, 'Let's pave that road,' and you start singing, 'Road, road, we're going to make a road.'"

The audience laughed. Doug was utterly plastered. The comedian stared at him and shook his head, grinning a bit.

"Jesus," he said. "I'm just going to avoid this side."

He looked out at the audience, still shaking his head.

"Is there anybody here as fucked up as this guy?" Everyone broke into applause and laughed. Doug laughed, too. The waitress came again.

"This is our last call," she said. "Do you want anything else?"

By then, I'd fallen behind. I had a full Coke sitting on the table.

"Another round," Doug said.

As we left, Doug gave me the keys to the car. He knew I wasn't supposed to drive. In this case, though, we both figured it would be safer with me behind the wheel.

When we got to the motel, Doug noticed a tavern, the Buoy Nine, across the street. The tavern looked ratty but Doug figured we could wander across and have a nightcap.

I was wearing down, but I was reluctant to show fatigue.

When we walked into the Buoy Nine I saw about ten shit-faced people. One guy had a guitar set up and was singing old Beatles and Jimmy Buffett songs. Next to him was an electric keyboard.

As we walked in, Doug walked up to a drunk stranger with

stringy blond hair. "Hey," Doug said, "my brother plays keyboard. He could jam along." He said it loud enough to be an announcement.

Doug turned to me.

"Come on. Go for it," he said.

"Nah," I said. "No way."

"Come on," he said. "You must know *something*."

"No," I said. "Really, I don't want to." Doug was making a bit of a scene.

"Yeah, but I told them you would," he said, full volume. "So if you don't, they're going to beat us up."

"Not now," I said, feeling utterly drained.

At the bar, Doug ordered a whiskey, a beer and a Coke. A guy came over and asked if we were going to "jam."

"Yeah," Doug said. Doug walked up behind the electric keyboard. Doug doesn't play piano. While the guy with the guitar sang, Doug started slapping away at the keys.

So I went up, pushed Doug aside and started playing along with the guitarist, watching his fingers to figure out the chords. Doug left the stage and walked over to a chunky blonde woman at the bar and asked her to dance. They stood in front of the stage, doing a kind of swing.

After the song was over, the guitarist asked me to sit in on another song. Doug stayed at the bar drinking and talking to the woman he'd been dancing with.

"That's great," Doug shouted after a song.

For the next two hours, I played the keyboard.

It was well after one o'clock when Doug said he was ready to leave. When we opened the door to leave, we walked smack into a North Carolina summer squall.

We ran toward our motel, but the rain came down so hard it bounced off the pavement. Doug ran underneath a covered bus stop, a dry ten-foot square, right across from the Buoy Nine.

When I reached the bus stop we stood there, awkward. I don't know if it's true for all brothers, but for Doug and me, talking can be tough. We have a fraternal bond that's everlasting. We've been friends and rivals. We've fought. But I've always loved Doug. He's my brother. My only brother.

As we stood there, I thought, "Doug's brother is dying." That's how I thought of it. I didn't think, "I'm dying." For me, this illness was refracted through the eyes of friends and loved ones.

I felt that my death would inflict pain upon my brother, a brother whom I would never hurt intentionally. Still, there's something in our chemistry that makes it hard for us to talk, to really *talk*.

As we stood soaking wet under the shelter, I knew we were both thinking about *it*. I had shoved it aside all day. Now, in the silence, in the dark, I could feel it there, hanging between us.

"Man," Doug said. "You were just jammin'."

Doug seemed to be groping for words. I didn't say anything.

"I mean it," Doug said. "I thought I was going to cry."

The rain was all around us. Doug seemed to be struggling to say something. But his words drifted all over the place.

"Man, what a great day," he said. "When I get out here with you two I feel so *free.* "

He was right. It was a great day. A crazy-great day. The kind of day you remember. The kind of day you laugh about years later. It was living. It was being brothers.

"I mean, NO MATTER WHAT," Doug said, emphasizing each word. He seemed almost angry. "*This was a great day.*"

"Sure was," I said.

"Man, you were just *jammin'*," he said. And he started to laugh. "I cried," he said. "I really cried."

There were no cars on the street. We stood in silence again.

"Sharon says you might have six years," Doug said out of the blue.

"Yeah, maybe," I said. "Nobody really knows."

"Yeah, but. . .wasn't *today* great?" Doug said. Doug seemed desperate and sad at the same time. "I mean, I don't *care*. I mean, you're just the *same*. All the girls were like, 'What's he going to be like?'"

I could picture them, my three sisters, wondering what Doug would find. Wondering what's happened to their big brother.

"I mean, you're *okay*," Doug said, and there was something in his voice that was heartbreaking. "I mean, you were in there *jammin'*. I mean, you're *just the same.* "

Doug put his arm around me. We stood for a moment, watching the rain.

"What a *great* day," he said.

Monday, August 17

Dear Emmy,

We came home from North Carolina exhausted. I collapsed on the couch. Doug collapsed, too. Mommy left to teach a class and soon after a friend, Ellie Fetterly, phoned. Ellie's husband, Mark, had just returned from a fishing trip. Mark, one of Virginia's only lobstermen, traps lobster off the continental shelf. Mark and Ellie were leaving town for a week and wanted to drop by three lobsters Mark brought home.

Around dinner time, Ellie arrived with a bag full of crab claws, a hunk of dolphin, and three lobsters in a paper bag. When Ellie came, you ran to the door. Ellie put down a paper bag and you looked inside.

"Look, Daddy," you shouted, "they're still alive." The lobsters were squirming around in the bag. "Can I see one?" you asked.

I reached into the bag and pulled out a lobster. The claws drooped a bit.

"Can I pet him?" you asked.

"Sure," I said. You rubbed your hand over the lobster's hard, bony back. You were excited. We'd eaten lobster before. The Fetterlys always have seafood around their house. Once Mark brought cases of rare golden crabs to someone's potluck and we ate until we our stomachs bloated out. Still, I'd never *cooked* lobster before. Lobster has always just sat on the plate, bright red, hot and ready to eat.

Now, I had this paper bag with three live lobsters. They had to be eaten or they'd die and go bad. The only way to cook them was to throw them into a pot of boiling water.

We didn't have a lobster pot so you and I walked to neighbors' homes to find a pot. You asked what I was looking for.

"A pot to cook the lobsters," I said.

"Don't cook them when they're *alive,* " you said.

I didn't know exactly what to say. I lied.

"They aren't alive anymore," I told you.

You got aggravated. "They're just *sleeping,* " you told me.

I changed the subject. That was fine with you. We got a large steel pot from the Joneses across the street. We came home and I filled the pot with water and put it on the stove. You stood in the kitchen watching.

"Daddy," you told me, "don't cook them when they're *real.* "

As the water in the pot started to warm up, I felt increasing dread about throwing live lobsters into the pot. Just as much, I was worried about what I'd say to you.

I'd never been very good about killing things. Doug either. When I was just nine years old, my dad started taking us to Kennedy Meadows in central California, to a remote stream we called Fish Creek. Some of my fondest memories were of nights at Fish Creek, lying in a sleeping bag next to my dad and my brother, gazing at the stars.

At Fish Creek we fished for rare golden trout caught in higher elevations of the Sierra Nevada range.

Those first years we used salmon eggs as bait. I remember threading a tiny hook into a salmon egg so precisely that it was totally embedded inside the egg's skin.

When we caught the trout, we gutted them and tossed them into a frying pan.

The trout died so suddenly. The trout came out of the stream frisky, flopping around. Moments later, their entrails were torn out and they sat cooked on a plate. The fish were considered a delicacy. I recall watching one of my dad's buddies pull a golden trout out of the frying pan, hold the tail, then lower the trout into his mouth, sucking off the meat, leaving a bare skeleton.

I never got over the idea that these fish were alive moments before, that we'd killed them—lots of them—just to have this dinner around the fire.

Over time, kids in our group got into killing other animals, too. Once a bunch of kids showed up at Fish Creek with BB guns. Some were pump action, others were powered by carbon dioxide cartridges. Someone came up with a game. We'd jump into the creek and wade upstream, as if on an expedition. Along the river lived mountain frogs, usually hidden in the muddy, overgrown banks, out of the sun. Every now and then we would spot a frog poking through. "There's one," someone would shout. He'd turn his BB gun toward the bank and fire away. If it was a good shot, the frog floated out, tugged from the underbrush by the current. The best shots hit the frogs between the eyes or on top of the head. You could see those BB shots on the frog's bodies, red spots showing through the green skin.

Another time, when I was probably 10 years old, our family took a train trip with my mom to her home town, Minto, North Dakota, to visit my granddad, Nigel. My brother and I hooked up with a group of kids. These kids fished in a brown stream that ran behind some of the homes. They usually caught catfish. Since nobody wanted to eat these, they caught them for the pleasure of it.

They killed them for pleasure, too. In the backyard of one house, near a big crab apple tree, somebody had set up a wooden plank, like a saw horse. It was covered with nail holes, hammer marks and dried guts. One time, on older kid caught a big catfish and laid it on the board. He pounded a nail through the catfish. The catfish, fastened by the long nail, slapped its tail on the board. The kid hammered in another nail, then another, then another. The fish kept flapping. Everybody laughed. We left the catfish there, nailed to the board, flapping for god knows how long.

But the image that sticks with me the most is the hummingbird. I remember once roaming with a pack of friends near my family's house in Southern California. We all had slingshots carved from tree branches. These were heavy-duty slingshots, armed with strips of inner tube. We walked around the neighborhood shooting cans or trees.

One day somebody spotted a bright green hummingbird. It hovered as it poked its snout into flowers. Someone in our group decided to have a contest: See who could hit the hummingbird. The hummingbird was so small, and our slingshots were so wild, we just chased it around. The hummingbird retreated into the branches of a tree in front of Mark Morganella's house. We all shot at it. The hummingbird ignored us. Then I grabbed a rock, put it into my slingshot and pulled back as hard as I could. I took aim and let go. My rock went right up to the tree branch. It skipped off the branch and glanced off the hummingbird's head.

"All right!" somebody shouted.

After hanging on for a few moments, the hummingbird dropped from the branch and landed in the gutter. We all went up to look. The hummingbird struggled in the gutter's mud. One wing moved. From its tiny green head dangled one black eyeball, the size of a BB. The image repulsed me. I shot this thing and now it lay in the gutter suffering.

But the hummingbird wouldn't *die*. It struggled to live. As it did everyone turned against me. *"You* shot it," somebody shouted. Now it was an accusation.

A friend and I decided to rescue the hummingbird. We picked it out of the gutter and tried to clean it off. I had a cage out in my backyard, near a sandbox. We put the hummingbird in the cage. The bird stood on a perch in the cage with its eye dangling.

I checked on the hummingbird until nightfall. In the morning, I went to check again. The cage was turned over. The door was opened. A cat had gotten to the cage in the dead of night.

Since those days, I've always shied away from anything that would seem unnecessarily cruel to animals. I've known people who are against killing any animal for any reason. That's fine. But that can be tough. Unfortunately, killing seems part of existing. Bugs kill each other. Birds kill each other. Bigger animals kill bugs and birds. Big fish eat small fish.

And humans have always killed. Here in our own home, we have spiders, ants, flies and, sometimes, termites. We kill them. Every now and then, a spider spins a web from our bedroom ceiling. Mommy will crush it and say, "I'm sorry I had to take your life."

Until this cancer episode, the notion of death and killing seemed comfortably remote. With the lobsters in my refrigerator, these memories came rushing back. These lobsters were *alive*. Presumably they wanted to live. How could you assume anything else? The only way to cook them was to drop them into a pot of boiling water.

There were alternatives. I could let them go. But really, that would kill them just the same. They lived in deep, cold water, miles offshore. Even if I built a lobster tank they'd just live a few days. The lobster squirming in my refrigerator were dead, really. There was no way to save them now. If I didn't have to put them in the pot myself, I probably wouldn't care how they died.

While the water boiled, you stood in the kitchen.

"Are the lobster still alive, Daddy?" you asked me.

"Emmy, why don't you go upstairs and color," I said. "I'll call you when dinner's ready." You left the kitchen.

I got the paper bag out of the refrigerator and grabbed a lobster. The easiest way to do this, I figured, was mechanically. Just put the lobster in the pot and set the dinner table.

I dropped one lobster in the boiling water. The lobster didn't squirm. It settled into the boiling water without twitching. I wondered: Is it still alive in there? Does it feel pain? Is it already dead? I took out the other lobster. I lowered it into the pot. It was too big. Its head wasn't under water. I shoved the lobster's head with a serving spoon. One of its tiny black eyes poked out of the water. I gave it another shove and the lobster settled in.

The lobster had long, red whiskers which protruded from the pot of boiling water. The whiskers moved slowly, as they had in the paper bag. I put the whiskers under the pot's lid and continued setting the table.

You came in and asked where the lobster were. I changed the subject. On top of everything else, you didn't need this. Death is death. Whether you're a lobster or a human. Somehow this whole process made death seem such a reality. It was there waiting. Whether I acknowledged it or not, death was *there* in the pot.

I served up lobster and fish and got ready to drop the third lobster into the pot.

"Daddy, he's *real,* " you said. "You can't cook him when he's *real.* " I put the lobster back in the refrigerator.

We all went into the dining room. You didn't seem to have any problem with the two cooked lobster sitting on the plate. "Are they dead?" you asked.

"Yes," I said.

You asked for a bite. You liked the lobster and I gave you several chunks. While you ate, I returned to the kitchen and cooked the third lobster.

Doug enjoyed the lobster but seemed disturbed about eating something that he'd seem squirming in the bottom of a paper sack just moments before.

"I love to eat prime rib," Doug said. "But I couldn't slaughter the cow myself."

Later that evening, I felt out of sorts. I don't know if it was the radiation or from eating so much lobster. I wondered what the hell I was doing, pretending that I wouldn't die. I know there's a difference between the life of a lobster and my life. Still, how could I say, "Death is normal, death is natural," and then decide it was normal and natural for everyone except me?

That evening I felt nauseous. Probably the radiation, I thought. Then I felt something going on in my brain. I felt pain up there. Actually, it was wasn't *really* pain. I felt as if my brain were somehow moving, as if a cockroach had wiggled underneath my skull. I wondered: What's happening in my brain? Is the tumor growing again? Is it possible to feel a tumor grow? Fears I'd worked so hard to banish flooded over me again.

Radiation.

Cancer.

Death.

By bedtime, I felt drained. I took you to bed, tucked you in and read you a story.

"Is that lobster still in the fridge?" you asked me as I got up to leave.

"No, Emmy, it's not there any more," I said.

"Did you kill it?" you asked me.

The question bothered me. I did kill it. That was the truth. But I couldn't tell you that. I just couldn't.

"No, hon," I said. "I let it go. I took it back to the ocean and let it go."

Dear Emmy,

Doug took me in for radiation treatment and an MRI to see what was happening with the blood clot in my brain. I came home with a pounding headache. I felt a deep, bone tiredness. I felt so tired my eyes couldn't focus. It reminded me a bit of driving at night, when you're struggling to keep awake.

After lunch, Doug made it clear that he was disgusted by the disorder in our kitchen.

"You ought to get a maid to come in once a week or so," Doug said.

"Yeah, well, we have maids come in every couple weeks," I said.

Doug gave me a strange look.

"What do they do?"

"Sweep, I guess."

"You ought to fire them."

Next time I walked into the kitchen, I saw that Doug had removed the doors from all our kitchen cabinets. He was cleaning grime out of the creases. He had also removed all our pots and pans and kitchen appliances.

"What you need is organization," he said. He showed me a drawer where everything was just tossed in.

"What's that?" he said.

"A junk drawer," I told him. He started pulling out the junk. He found a bottle of Grecian Formula Number Nine and a tube of denture adhesive that somebody had given me for my thirtieth birthday.

"What are these for?" he said.

I told him they were gag gifts.

"Why are you keeping them?"

"I thought I'd save it for a joke gift for somebody else, you know, turning 40."

"Yeah, and you'd know right where to find it."

He looked at the stove, took it apart. He removed the cover on the exhaust fan and spooned off the grease. "That's just like bacon," he said.

"I'm tired," I told Doug. "I'm going to lie down for about an hour." I went upstairs but I couldn't sleep at all. My head pounded. I turned over. The other side throbbed.

What the hell was going on inside my head?

That's the worse thing about illness. The uncertainty, the fact that you go through long stretches without any idea what's happening inside your body.

I was miserable. I held a pillow over my head. Eventually, I drifted off. I pretty much slept the day away. When I awoke, Doug was still downstairs cleaning and "organizing" our kitchen. I went to join him and we worked together through the evening.

Dear Emmy,

Mommy and I went to see my neurosurgeon today so he could examine my MRIs to determine if the blood clot in my brain had grown. If it were growing, I'd probably have to go through surgery again. I didn't want that. Mommy didn't want that.

He would also look for any sign of tumor growth. If my tumor were extremely malignant it might have begun to grow back already.

We waited in the neurosurgeon's examining room for a long time. I could hear his voice, muffled, as he talked to a patient in another room. What was he saying? What did the patient have? So much bad news delivered in one small office.

When Dr. Partington walked into the room, he seemed cheerful.

"Have you seen the MRIs?" he asked. He escorted us to a hallway where about a dozen MRIs hung against a wall of fluorescent light. Dr. Partington said it appeared that the blood clot had almost entirely vanished.

He pointed to the brain scan.

"This is where the tumor was debulked," he said pointing to a black cavity in the brain. "This," he said, pointing at a bright white line surrounding the cavity, "This looks like normal scar tissue. The radiologist and I looked at it and we both agreed that it appeared to be normal scar tissue."

I felt a sense of relief. The blood clot no longer existed. There would be no surgery. There was no evidence that the tumor had returned.

We went back to Dr. Partington's office. I asked what would happen next. He told me that once I finished radiation, I'd probably be through with doctors for a while. After three months, I'd return for my first follow-up MRI. He'd then compare the newest MRIs to the ones just taken. If there were any sign of tumor growth, he'd go in and take out the tumor. "We'll be as aggressive as possible," he said.

During our earlier visits, he made it clear that the tumor *was* going to return at some point. Now, as we sat in the office, Dr. Partington talked about what we'd do "when the tumor came back, if ever."

Two words. *If ever.* Did he mean them? Was he serious?

Mommy and I both clung to those words, but didn't ask for clarification, because we didn't *want* clarification. As we walked across the parking lot toward our car, I turned to Mommy.

"*If ever,* " I told Mommy. "He said, '*If ever.*'"

"I heard that," Mommy said.

"He never said that before," I told Mommy. "He's never said, '*If ever.*' He's always said, '*When*'."

"I know," Mommy said. "Maybe the radiation is killing it all. Maybe you'll be one of those rare cures."

We got into the car and drove home. In the car, Mommy began to cry with relief. It was clear and cool, the best weather we'd had since Doug arrived. As we drove home, I watched other people in the cars all around us, people heading to and from work, doing chores. I sat in the passenger's seat and thought about those two words. If ever.

"The blood clot's gone," I told Mommy. "No surgery. It's just gone."

I had worked so hard to be upbeat for so long.

"I don't know if I could have taken any more bad news," I told Mommy.

"I know," Mommy said.

"I really don't," I told her. "It's *so hard.* "

I turned away and looked out the passenger's window, choking up.

If ever, he'd said. *If ever.*

Dear Emmy,

Doug flew home yesterday. As he got ready to leave, I felt a sense of desperation. Whether knowingly or not, Doug kept me doing things—cleaning, organizing, traveling, always moving, not allowing exhaustion and depression to suck me down. It was hard for me to express how grateful I was that he came, and how much I wanted him to stay. But he had to go home.

As soon as he left, I felt the energy drain. Today, I felt more exhausted than I ever have in my life. Not physically tired. Brain tired. It felt as if my brain had been assaulted, bruised, tormented.

Without Doug here, I felt so alone in our home, depressed, scared of dying. This morning, I walked into the bathroom and looked in the mirror. I could see scaly patches of dying skin where radiation had scorched my scalp. I could see that swollen, red scar. I was disfigured. Forever.

All day long, I suffered waking nightmares about what might happen to me. We have a picture in your room taken the day we adopted you. I remember taking that picture in the first hour you came into our life. Now, as I walked by, I couldn't stop these powerful waves of emotion. I looked at all the pictures on our wall. Pictures of you smiling. Pictures of you in my arms. Pictures of us walking through castle courtyards in Wales.

Why? Why was this happening?

When I started to write these letters, I had one purpose in mind. I wanted you to know me. To understand me. But my life seems to have exploded before my eyes. I can't focus on anything anymore. I seem to be drifting, winding down. Dying.

Today I decided to write you a children's story. Something you could understand *now*.

I spent the day writing you this story:

The Secret of the Mango Tree

Once upon a time, deep in the jungle, lived three caterpillars, Poppa, Momma, and Baby Jade.

The three caterpillars loved the jungle. They loved the birds and the bushes and the trees and the vines. And they loved each other.

They loved each other so much that Poppa Caterpillar always called them "the three caterpillar musketeers."

"Poppa," Baby Jade said. "You're the funnest caterpillar in the jungle."

One day, Poppa Caterpillar felt strange.

"Momma and Baby Jade," Poppa said. "I have to climb that mango tree."

"No you don't," Momma said. But Poppa Caterpillar couldn't help himself.

"When will you be back, Poppa?" Baby Jade asked.

"I don't know," Poppa answered.

"Please, stay here in the jungle with us," Baby Jade pleaded. "Don't you love us?"

"I love you more than words can say, Baby Jade," said Poppa. "But I can't help myself. I have to climb that mango tree."

While Momma and Baby Jade watched, Poppa slowly inched up the mango tree. Poppa fastened himself to a branch and wrapped his body in fibers until he was completely encased in a cocoon.

Baby Jade sobbed. "Poppa's gone!" she said.

Momma broke down, too, as she watched her best buddy vanish.

Baby Jade and Momma crawled off into the jungle, mourning the loss of their third musketeer.

"Will Poppa ever come back?" Baby Jade asked.

"I don't think so," Momma said.

Soon after, Momma and Baby Jade noticed a butterfly fluttering near them. It was a beautiful butterfly, red, blue, green and yellow. They couldn't talk to the butterfly, but wherever Momma and Baby Jade went the butterfly followed.

Momma and Baby Jade and the butterfly lived in the jungle for years. Baby Jade befriended a young caterpillar and began her own family. She had her own daughter, Kiki. Momma loved seeing Baby Jade so happy.

One day Momma Caterpillar felt strange.

"Baby Jade," she said. "I have to climb that mango tree."

Baby Jade burst into tears.

"Please, Momma," she begged. "Don't climb that mango tree! Remember what happened to Poppa?"

"I'm sorry," Momma said. "I can't help myself."

Momma inched up the mango tree and called back, "Baby Jade, I love you."

Baby Jade's heart was broken. She watched through tears as Momma wrapped herself into a cocoon.

"First my Poppa, now my Momma," she said. "Life is so sad."

Baby Jade crawled off into the jungle weeping. Kiki tried to comfort her. But Baby Jade knew that someday she'd have to climb the mango tree, too—and leave Kiki behind.

A few days later, Momma Caterpillar emerged from her cocoon. Momma wasn't a caterpillar anymore. She was the most beautiful butterfly in the jungle.

As she fluttered from her cocoon, she spotted the butterfly that had followed her all those years.

"Poppa!" she called out.

They fluttered through the jungle together and found Baby Jade.

Baby Jade eventually noticed another butterfly fluttering nearby. That butterfly followed her, too, though they could never talk.

Momma and Poppa Butterfly watched as Baby Jade raised her own family, as Kiki grew fat and strong. They also saw, late at night, that Baby Jade cried alone because she missed Momma and Poppa Caterpillar so much.

Sometimes Momma and Poppa tried to comfort her. They fluttered around her and did tricks. Momma found out she could talk to Baby Jade, but only in dreams. Baby Jade could never believe those dreams of talking butterflies.

It hurt Momma and Poppa to watch their baby girl cry. They ached to wipe away her tears. They ached to tell Baby Jade what they knew.

They ached to tell Baby Jade the secret of the mango tree. The secret of the cocoon.

They ached to tell Baby Jade that someday, when she inched up that mango tree herself, they'd be waiting there for her.

That, on that day, they would all fly together.

At bedtime, I read you three books—*The Cat in the Hat, Madeline's Rescue,* and *The Fox and the Hound.*

Then I told you I wanted to read my own story. As I started, you liked the part about the caterpillars. When Poppa caterpillar climbed the mango tree and made his cocoon, you said: "Why is he making the cocoon?"

"Well, caterpillars always make cocoons."

"I don't want to hear about the cocoon," you told me. "Read the story, but don't read about the cocoon."

"But the story. . .I don't have to finish the story."

"Read the story, but not the cocoon."

I started to read on. But I realized this was impossible. How could I tell a story about butterflies without mentioning a cocoon?

When I read to the part about Mommy climbing the mango tree, you said: "Why is she climbing the mango tree?"

"Well. . ."

"No more. I don't like this story. Don't read any more."

"But, Emmy, they turn into beautiful butterflies."

"I don't want to hear this story."

I lay there next to you. Then you looked up at me. Your eyes were full of tears. I felt my heart break. What the hell was I thinking? You leaned onto my chest, hugged me, and started to sob. I couldn't keep you from crying.

"I love you so much, Emmy," I said, stoking your head. But you couldn't stop yourself. "I love you *so* much."

Friday, August 28

Dear Emmy,

This morning I had a dream.

I was in the radiation room at DePaul Hospital. Kim and Lisa, the technicians who have treated me every day, were going through their routine. They set up laser beams and the linear accelerator. When they finished, Kim said, "Just a second. We aren't done yet."

The room went dark. Colored lights started flashing. Somebody cranked up the music. This was some kind of celebration. It was a graduation ceremony. I had graduated from radiation.

Two more treatments. A Friday, then this coming Monday.

Two more treatments.

When I went in to the hospital this morning, I lay down on the radiation table.

"I had a dream about you two," I said to Kim and Lisa.

They both laughed.

"What were we doing?" asked Kim. "Tying you down?"

"No. It was my last day. I saw lights and music. It was like a graduation ceremony."

They both laughed. Another tech walked in. They joked about getting me a gown and a diploma for graduating.

"He can't wear a cap during treatment," one said, "and I'm sure he doesn't want a hospital gown."

After treatment, on most Fridays, Mommy and I meet with the doctor.

"You can skip meeting him today," Kim told me. "You have to see him your last day anyway. Graduation day."

When I walked out, I told the nurse at the front desk that I'd be skipping my visit with the doctor since I'd be seeing him my last day.

"Oh," she said. "Graduation day."

My friends and relatives have been excited. Just a few days before, a friend told me, "You've only got ten days left." In my mind, I worked out the mathematics. Ten days of a 30-day treatment is one third. One *third!* With radiation accumulating during each treatment. "Just ten more days" didn't comfort me. It scared me to death. I'd think, "I've done this well so far. I'm still coherent. I've had no seizures. I can walk. Why not stop now?"

But now, I had one more day.

One more day.

Now, with just one more day I'm not worried at all. Nothing's going to happen. I'm going to walk in Monday, get my treatment. The doctor will wave me off. It will be over.

People always ask me, "Were the treatments effective?" Truth is, nobody knows. Doctors, for the most part, perform all their medical magic in the dark. Then they send you off.

So long.

You're on your own now.

When I came home from radiation yesterday, the end seemed tangible. I was almost done. Since the end of treatments seemed so near, and the exhaustion seemed so complete, I decided to quit fighting it. I'd spend the weekend relaxing. Next week, with the radiation complete, I'd begin to get my life in order again.

So I spent a good part of the day hanging around the house, playing piano, writing, talking to friends on the phone.

In the afternoon, you and I walked to 7-Eleven. You've gotten to love these trips to 7-Eleven. We always leave Mommy behind. We wander. We stop. We make detours.

During this trip, I took your kite, a plastic triangle with a unicorn. A storm was rolling in as we walked. Wind gusted from every direction—north, east, west. Whenever I felt a gust, I threw your kite into the air. It shot up, tethered by a short string, sometimes circling around you as the wind changed. Then the wind would die and the kite would waft to the ground. We spent probably an hour, walking, flying kites, sitting, talking.

By the time we got home from 7-Eleven a tremendous thunderstorm had rolled in. There were flashes of lightning and booms of thunder. Winds must have gusted up to 60 miles an hour.

"Get some rest," Mommy told me. I knew Mommy and I were supposed to go out tonight. I went upstairs and fell asleep. I don't know how long I slept. Ten minutes? Two hours? I had no notion.

For the first time in a week, I woke feeling rested. The storm outside had cleared. Although there were still clouds and wind, the rain seemed to have passed.

Mommy was ironing clothes for both of us. She seemed excited about going out together. I put on my freshly ironed clothes and wore my white Dobbs straw hat. The sitter came and I kissed you goodbye.

As we walked out of the house, I was struck by how beautiful the night was. Even the clouds looked spectacular, a mishmash of white and gray illuminated by the moon. I knew the storm that had passed might come back.

"Let's still walk," I told Mommy.

"Sure," Mommy said. She didn't seem worried about having to walk back in a downpour.

I felt exhilarated. I did most of the talking. As we walked, fresh, cold rainwater dripped from the trees onto my bare forearms. We ducked under rain-soaked crepe myrtle branches. I brushed soggy pink flowers from my hat's brim. I enjoyed looking down at the moss growing between the sidewalk cracks. There was so much of it and it seemed so green, struggling up through the concrete.

I had no notion of how my life was going to turn out. I had no notion whether I'd live months or years. But I was determined at least to savor this day.

"You want to eat in the bar?" I asked Mommy when we walked through the restaurant's doorway.

"No," she said. "I really want to eat in the restaurant."

She turned to a young guy wearing a snug, black tuxedo. She told him she had reservations.

"Reservations?" I thought. "You don't need reservations here." I could see empty tables all over the place.

As we walked into the restaurant, I saw a long table. A group of about 30 people. I saw someone I recognized from the newspaper. "Damn," I thought. I figured this was some newspaper focus group out for an evening meeting.

Then I saw neighbors at the table. Friends. People from church who had brought me food over the past four months. Ellie and Mark Fetterly. This gathering didn't make any sense.

What were these people doing together? What was going on? What was the connection?

Then it dawned on me. I was the connection. Everyone looked at me. This was arranged. Mommy did this. I was too stunned to act surprised.

This was my graduation party.

Tuesday, December 1

Dear Emmy,

It's winter now. Three months have passed since that sweltering August day I had my last radiation treatment.

Just a few days after I finished, you celebrated your fourth birthday. I still felt exhausted, but I had enough energy to tie balloons to the fence, cut the cake, take photographs, and sing Happy Birthday.

Two months after treatment, I flew to California to see my brother Doug, my mother, and my three sisters. I had talked to them on the phone dozens of times, but nothing compared to being with them, staying up late talking, remembering, laughing.

Last week, I had to go for my first follow-up MRI, the three-month check-up to see if the tumor had returned.

Today I went to see Dr. Partington to get the result.

Going back to the hospital wasn't easy. For three months, I had avoided doctors and hospitals altogether. I dreaded going back.

When I went in for the MRI, I had to walk past all those familiar signs—Oncology, Radiology, Surgery, Intensive Care. I felt dread I hadn't known in months. As I walked toward the MRI room, the public address system calmly delivered pages for doctors and nurses, all in "codes," so as not to alarm.

"Code blue," I heard, and wondered, "What *is* code blue?" For me, for others in the hospital, it was better not to know.

As I was eased into the MRI, its throat seemed even narrower than I remembered. The MRI brought back a flood of purposefully repressed memories. I had forgotten how much I hated that white, placid-looking medical miracle. That monster. I lay inside the MRI scanner for an hour, wondering whether technicians could see any sign of tumor growth. A sliver of white, no larger than a nail clipping, could change the course of my existence.

This morning, when Mommy and I sat in Dr. Partington's office, my overwhelming fear was that I'd be sucked back permanently into this world of medicine, hospitals, surgery, tests. Mommy and I sat anxiously, praying for my doctor's consent to return to our lives.

Last spring, before all this happened, I imagined life spread before me like an endless rolling landscape. Now, my life is parceled out in three-month intervals. The reality of returning every three months for an MRI, another verdict, casts a mist over the future.

When doctors say you have an 80-percent chance of dying in surgery, fears can overwhelm. Fears are probably just as intense if you have a 20-percent chance of dying in surgery. After surgery, though, doctors declare an operation successful.

With a chronic illness, especially illnesses that are often terminal, nobody wheels out a gurney to pronounce the patient "saved." It's like being trapped forever in the waiting room, waiting for word that will never come.

How long will I live? Eighteen months? Eight years? Eighteen years? Nobody can tell me. Today, I reside in a waiting room with millions of others who have cancer, AIDS, or heart disease. We gather, fearful but hoping, with a concrete sense of mortality accompanying our every moment; yet, at the same time, appreciating the magic and majesty of life.

These days, I look at friends I've known for years, who've never suffered any health problems, and I can see that they, too, are in the same waiting room. They just don't know it.

Dr. Partington walked in the examination room seeming upbeat. The radiologist, he said, had seen "no evidence of tumor recurrence." Relief rushed over me, coursed through my veins. My guts unwound.

The MRI was *perfect*, Partington said, without any trace that would require a judgment call. As far as he could tell, my tumor was gone. At least for now. He gave me an exam and acted surprised to see that my hair had slowly begun to grow back.

The meeting didn't last long. He obviously had more pressing matters. I felt grateful to be sloughed off, not to be one of the pressing matters that required urgent attention.

Mommy and I walked from his office holding hands, gazing teary-eyed at the rich, wonderful world around us. I could *leave*. Go home. Go hold you in my arms.

The mist had cleared for at least another three months. I've begun to dare to look farther ahead. Maybe, just maybe, I'll be a part of your life, Emmy. Maybe I'll be able to place that gold locket on your neck on your thirteenth birthday.

Still, over these seven months, I've grown vividly aware that life offers no extra days or second chances. Like many, I once felt comfortable sacrificing today, and tomorrow, a week, maybe a year, in the hopes of something better in a cloudy future. I could sleepwalk through life for months at a time. Now I sense how wasted moments and wasted hours get woven into wasted lives.

I don't know how much time I have remaining. But, short or long, I know it's a lifetime. My lifetime. To be *lived*.

Postscript: Two years after his diagnosis, Greg Raver-Lampman and his family have returned from living for a year in the Czech Republic, where his wife taught in a university on a Fulbright Scholars award. Raver-Lampman left the newspaper and has completed his second book, a novel entitled White Tribes.

Greg Raver Lampman attended the American College in Paris, Pepperdine University, and received a B. A. in Comparative Literature from the University of California at Berkeley. He and his wife Sharon spent two years in Ecuador and Jamaica for the Peace Corps. After returning he wrote for newspapers and magazines including the *St. Petersburg Times*, the *Tampa Tribune, Spy, Regardie's,* and for the *Virginian-Pilot and The Ledger-Star.* He has received: numerous awards for feature writing series and in-depth reporting; Black Media Professionals "Echoes of Excellence" and has received two nominations for a Pulitzer Prize. He has traveled extensively both here and abroad. He now lives with his family in Norfolk, Virginia, where he is completing his first novel, *White Tribes.*

Ha   ical,

Woul   area of
int   call
t   to: